P9-EEU-634

Guide for
Mental Health Workers

by
Armando R. Favazza, M.D.
Barbara Starks Favazza, M.D.
and Philip M. Margolis, M.D.

ANN ARBOR
THE UNIVERSITY OF MICHIGAN PRESS

Contents

Foreword

In 1916, Sigmund Freud lamented that ". . . our therapeutic activities are not very far reaching. There are only a handful of us . . . who can help only a small number of patients, compared to the vast amount of neurotic misery which there is in the world." Perhaps Freud was prophesying the eventual development of the mental health worker.

Over the years various organizations have been aided and enriched by the services of persons who were not professionally trained and some special programs have been developed. Probably the best known and most significant was the long term program for psychotic patients in Gheel, Belgium, which established a high reputation for nonprofessional participation in the care of the mentally ill.

With the extraordinary demand for assistance in the mental health field, with the growing field of community mental health and with the comparatively small number of professionals, such as psychiatrists, psychologists, and social workers,

available even today, it seems not only appropriate but imperative that we begin training interested citizens to fill definitive roles and functions.

There are many books and articles on other
types of programs, but practically nothing in the
literature dealing with the activities and training
of pre- or para- professional workers. In fact,
there are no specific guidelines for what and how
to teach them. This monograph, therefore, is an
important contribution to the field of community
mental health in particular and of psychiatry in
general.

Raymond W. Waggoner, M.D.

Preface

Community Psychiatry is a point of view. One of its primary thrusts is to tap new sources in order to reduce the tremendous mental health manpower shortage. There are a number of lay (non-mental health) people in this country who are interested in and sensitive to certain mental health problems, and potentially capable of handling them. This book is for these people.

The book was the idea of a first-year resident in psychiatry, Dr. Armando Favazza, who obtained part of his community psychiatry training via a three-month experience at the Washtenaw County Community Mental Health Center. There he came in contact with a group of mental health workers who themselves were being trained to man a crisis telephone service. The workers encouraged him and his wife, Dr. Barbara Favazza, who also trained at the Center, to write them something readable. They did. I supervised, taught, edited, did a little rewriting, and "inspired."

Our thanks go to the Center and Community Psychiatry staff, especially to Sue Cox who typed the initial draft and to Dinah Arnold who completed the task. Finally, I am indebted to Dr. Raymond Waggoner, Chairman, Department of Psychiatry, for his helpful and generous support in this endeavor.

Philip M. Margolis, M.D.

Introduction

Laymen have long had a profound interest in mental health and mental illness, perhaps because there is scarcely an individual who has not personally come into contact with a relative or friend suffering from schizophrenia, alcoholism, chronic organic brain syndrome, or painful neurosis. Laymen have been important in influencing mental health legislation, raising funds for mental health programs, and performing occasional volunteer duties at mental health facilities.

With the birth of the community mental health movement, laymen have been encouraged to engage in direct patient care as well as indirect services such as education and research. "Mental health worker" is the name applied to interested, voluntary laymen working in community mental health facilities. Laymen now interview clients,*

*The word 'client' is a poor one for our purposes and will rarely be used in this book. It applies to a person who asks a lawyer for advice or who is receiving the services of a social welfare agency, government bureau, and the like. Similarly the word 'patient' seems inappropriate unless it designates a person seen by a physician. The mental health worker may see potential patients. Mostly he sees people.

1

act as their advocates (the "indigenous worker" concept), help with brief therapy and crisis intervention, act as semiofficial spokesmen to civic and other groups, and engage actively in epidemiological studies.

Since the Washtenaw County Community Mental Health Center came into existence two years ago, more than fifty mental health workers have been trained. Most of these workers are women from the local community. Many of them had no training in psychology or social work. They were simply interested in helping the mentally ill and in promoting the ideals of mental health. These workers form an integral part of the Center. They interview clients by telephone and in person; they help staff the Crisis Walk-In Clinic; they intervene in crises under close supervision; they make home visits; they help to organize community mental health projects; they have been instrumental in gathering data and in helping to formulate programs for the better delivery of mental health services.

The majority of their training is on the job. They do, however, have an important orientation period in which they are taught interviewing techniques, mental health concepts, the use of community resources, methods of intervention in times of crisis, etc.

At the early stages of their training, the workers have repeatedly asked for written materials.

Introduction

We researched the literature and made available a collection of pertinent articles. The difficulty with this was that the articles were written for psychiatrists, psychologists, and social workers. They were filled with jargon and often had much material extraneous to a mental health worker's needs. We then decided to produce written material for the workers. The outcome of our decision is this book.

We have attempted to produce what the workers asked for—a short, simple, pertinent manual. It is meant to be read quickly and also to be used as a handy reference. It covers the following material:

1. Overview of Mental Disease and Treatment. Here we present basic concepts and commonly used terminology so that the mental health worker can develop a general idea of what mental illness is, how it is classified, and what treatment involves.
2. Stresses of Everyday Life. This informational chapter discusses common stresses that accompany the adolescent period, marriage and family life, working, aging, etc.
3. The Concept of Community Mental Health. We set community mental health into a brief historical perspective

and explain the services that a community mental health center provides.

4. The Interview. We outline the techniques of interviewing.

5. Suicide. Mental health workers have consistently been anxious about this topic. In this chapter we offer some assurance that a mental health worker can learn to handle a suicidal client properly by picking up certain cues.

6. Alcoholism and Drug Abuse. These mental health problems are ubiquitous and frequently involve many agencies. We write about Alcoholics Anonymous as this is a frequently used and often misunderstood resource.

7. Community Resources and Programs in Prevention. Here we discuss the most common community facilities and the programs with which the mental health worker will probably come into contact. Brief clinical vignettes are presented.

It is our hope that upon reading this book a mental health worker would be well prepared to undertake a training and orientation program. The book may also be used as a brief text for such a program. By first comprehending the general situation, the worker may then focus on the details. Although primary training takes place on the job, this book may help make the job more meaningful and less filled with agonizing surprises and false expectations.

1 Overview of Mental Disease and Treatment

The purpose of this chapter is to provide you with a general introduction to the concepts of mental illness and its treatment. You will probably hear professionals use words such as "psychosis" or "neurosis." You need not memorize definitions or become concerned with the diagnosis a professional makes. For your own interest, however, some background information may be helpful.

A *psychosis* is a serious mental disorder because it is characterized by poor contact with reality. The psychotic person has difficulty distinguishing between what goes on in the real world and what goes on in his mind.

Schizophrenia is a form of psychosis. There are many different symptoms of this illness and only rarely will a schizophrenic person have them all. Some schizophrenics are severely disturbed, others mildly so. Schizophrenics may have episodes of noticeable illness, while between the episodes they may appear to be relatively normal.

Some schizophrenics remain noticeably disturbed for long periods of time and require constant care, while other chronic schizophrenics are relatively self-sufficient and may hold "routine," or simple jobs. There are many schizophrenics who are office workers, laborers, skilled teachers, artists, professionals, etc.

Typical of schizophrenia is an abnormal way of thinking. The schizophrenic's thoughts are frequently not connected in a logical fashion. He may invent new words. His conversation may not make much sense to the listener.

Schizophrenics may have false beliefs (delusions) and be unable to heed reason. They may feel that they are being persecuted and that people are laughing at them. They may feel that everyday events have mysterious meanings for them, e.g., a passing car may be a secret signal. Sometimes they may hallucinate, hearing voices which do not actually exist, except in their own minds.

Socially, many schizophrenics tend to be withdrawn and are loners. They do not communicate well with others. If the disorder progresses, their personal hygiene may deteriorate and they may develop odd habits, such as collecting junk or garbage.

Schizophrenics often fail to show appropriate feelings or emotions. As an example, they may feel happy and laugh under circumstances when a normal person would feel quite sad.

Paranoid schizophrenics have many delusions. They often feel they are being persecuted,
that they have special powers, or that they are
someone else, such as Jesus or the President. Some
may come to the community's attention because
of their attempts to gain satisfaction for supposed
wrongs done to them.

What causes schizophrenia? Schizophrenia
may be due to complex psychological conflict
and/or chemical changes in the brain. The exact
cause is not yet known.

The treatment of schizophrenia revolves
around drugs and psychotherapy. Treatment may
include helping the schizophrenic to meet and
work with other people through recreational and
occupational therapy. It is necessary to maintain
a trustful, truthful attitude towards schizophrenics. With proper treatment some recover; some
do well and return to normal life even though
they have certain symptoms; some remain rather
dependent and have obvious personality defects,
but can live in society; and a few either get pro-
gressively worse or reach a stable state requiring
permanent help. At times a schizophrenic's con-
dition may worsen. These episodes are often un-
predictable. If they are discovered early enough,
prompt drug treatment and psychotherapy may
prevent hospitalization.

Schizophrenics ought to be hospitalized if
they are suicidal, abusive, very frightened, or being taken advantage of by others. Hospitalization

is often in the best interest of the patient and of society because the schizophrenic may not be in complete contact with reality and, therefore, not responsible for his actions. The removal of environmental pressure may prompt a speedy recovery. It must be emphasized that many schizophrenics never come into psychiatric care and that the vast majority are living fairly well in the community.

People under the influence of powerful drugs, such as LSD, are in many ways like schizophrenics. They are psychotic—see visions, hear voices, and think abnormally. Sometimes the fear that schizophrenics feel is also felt by the drug user. Not all experiences with psychedelic ("mind expanding") or hallucination-producing drugs are pleasant ones.

Another type of psychosis is *severe depression*. Typically, the psychotic, depressed person holds a firm, false belief that he is an unworthy person who deserves "punishment." He is burdened with great guilt. He is a bleak person with a bleak outlook on life. Often he sees no solution but suicide. If he is agitated, the risk of suicide is high.

Talking with a severely depressed person is like trying to pull nails from concrete. He will usually sigh, think and talk very slowly, and look very sad. His mind and body slow down.

What causes psychotic depression? Certain individuals suffer such a depression following a

9

loss of someone or something important. Examples of such losses are the death of a loved one, financial disaster, or retirement.

Treatment with antidepressant drugs is often effective. Electroshock therapy often rapidly clears up such depressions also. Psychotherapy helps the patient to regain his self-esteem.

In some individuals periods of extreme excitement and activity called *mania* alternate with periods of depression. A *manic* person is excessively active, speaks rapidly, jokes a great deal, is alive with energy, and is flighty. He feels "so good" that he may undertake fantastic tasks and deplete his finances. This type of illness, known as manic-depressive psychosis, seems to run in families. Usual treatment consists of drug therapy for the excitement, electroshock therapy or drugs for the depression, and psychotherapy throughout.

The *neuroses* are probably the most common form of mental illness. Neurotic individuals are in good contact with reality, but their minds are often upset with fears, feelings of inferiority, desires to punish and to be punished, feelings of guilt, and other disturbing thoughts. They are often preoccupied with thoughts of themselves. They deal with many different situations in the same, inflexible way. Neurotic people are often unhappy. Their "hangups" make it difficult for them to enjoy life and to function productively.

What causes neuroses? A commonly accepted theory is that development of a neurosis may begin when a situation or thought causes a person to feel anxious. Severe anxiety may result from conflicting conscious and unconscious thoughts, wishes, and feelings. Anxiety is very unpleasant and most neurotic symptoms are attempts to avoid anxiety. All of this occurs unconsciously so that the person is not aware of what is happening.

The experience of *anxiety* itself is a feeling of dread and a fear of the unknown. An anxious person may feel pounding of his heart, tense muscles (tense head muscles can cause "tension headache"), sweating, dry mouth, or faintness. A person suffering from chronic anxiety may be said to have an anxiety neurosis.

Mental defenses are mechanisms, unconsciously selected and automatically operated, designed to allay anxiety. Defense mechanisms are normally used by everyone in daily life. When anxiety is severe, as in some mental illnesses, these mechanisms operate so that symptoms may be formed to decrease anxiety. Among the more common defense mechanisms are repression, denial, projection, displacement, turning against the self, reaction formation, rationalization, and intellectualization.

In *repression* an unpleasant wish, impulse, or feeling is relegated to the unconscious portions

11

of the mind. Thus a person may not be able to remember easily something which was painful. If repression is totally successful a person will experience no anxiety and may have no symptoms.

Denial consists of the mind's refusal to acknowledge an experience. An example might be a person who is so terrified at the presence of a physical illness that he denies its existence. Of course, he does not do this consciously. He may be quite surprised if someone points out the obvious illness to him.

Projection is a mechanism in which an individual attributes his own thoughts and feelings to another person. For example, an angry man may project his anger onto his wife and feel that she is angry with him.

Displacement involves the switching of an emotion from one idea or object to another similar idea or object. For example, an angry man who projects his anger onto his gray-haired wife may displace the anger onto gray cats.

In *turning-against-the-self* an individual places feelings meant for other people back onto himself. For example, a woman disappointed in her husband may come to feel disappointed in herself.

Rationalization occurs when a person unconsciously tries to explain logically his thoughts, feelings, and actions in an attempt to hide the true motives for his behavior.

A person employing the defense of *intellectualization* avoids emotional interactions with others by talking circumstantially and aloofly. For example, in response to the question, "Do you love your child?" a woman might intellectualize and spend ten minutes presenting pro and con arguments.

Defense mechanisms are utilized by the mind to ward off anxiety. Ordinarily, the results of the defense operations are not noticeable. With a neurosis, however, the symptoms indicate which defenses are being used. One does not consciously determine which defense to use. As stated before, the deployment of a defense is automatic and unconscious. Its selection depends upon the type of person and life experiences of that person.

The following are some types of neuroses:

1. A *phobia* is an abnormal fear. A phobic person unconsciously places his anxiety onto some external object, such as cats or elevators. Then, by fearing and therefore avoiding cats or elevators, he can avoid anxiety.
2. *Amnesia* is a loss of interrelated memories in a person without a brain injury. An amnesic person may not remember who he is.
3. A *conversion* neurosis is one in which psychological conflict is converted into

13

a physical symptom. An example might be a bride who has conflicts about sex, develops a mysterious weakness of the legs, and thus cannot walk down the aisle to get married.

4. *Hypochondriasis* is excessive complaining about bodily pains which have no physical basis.

5. Neurotic *depressions* are not as severe as psychotic depressions. The individual experiences feelings of dejection and worthlessness and often complains of bodily pain.

6. An *obsessive compulsive* neurosis is one in which a person is obsessed with certain repetitive thoughts and feels compelled to perform rituals. As an example, such an individual may feel it necessary to wash his hands over and over or to count and recount telephone poles in order to decrease anxiety.

Treatment of neuroses consists primarily of psychotherapy which attempts to unravel the present-day as well as the childhood sources of the anxiety. Drugs may also be helpful in decreasing anxiety.

Another large group of mental illnesses are called *personality* disorders. People with these disorders have deep-seated, unusual personality trends which may not be disturbing to them. Such individuals may not be uncomfortable and therefore may have little motivation to change themselves.

One type of personality disorder is characterized by consistent coldness, aloofness, and seclusiveness. Persons with another type of personality disorder may be overly suspicious and stubborn. In a third type, individuals may easily and rapidly change from moods of sadness to happiness and back again. Obsessive compulsive individuals may be perfectionistic, tense, and overly conscientious. A person with a passive-aggressive personality is one who may combine traits of helplessness (passivity) with displays of temper tantrums, pouting, and stubbornness (forms of aggressiveness).

More serious forms of personality disturbances may be found in people who are out of step with society's rules. Jails are full of such people—for example, chronic car stealers or check forgers. They usually do not consider themselves ill, yet they do not learn from experience. Upon release from jail they often go back to their old ways. Sexual deviates may also have personality disorders. Homosexuality is the most common deviation. Since deviates frequently do not desire to change, treatment is often not successful. Alcoholics and drug addicts are also considered to have personality disturbances.

Another large group of mental disorders are called *brain syndromes*. These are disorders in which brain tissue is not functioning properly, producing symptoms.

A person with damaged brain tissue may be confused and may not know where he is, who he is, the date, or the time. He may become irritable, jealous, distrustful, and somewhat childlike. He may neglect personal hygiene, lose ambition, and lack sympathy for others. Depression and suicidal thoughts are frequent.

What are the common causes of damage to brain tissue? Old people frequently develop such damage because the arteries to their brain become hard and narrow and no longer allow enough blood to reach the brain. In other cases a diseased heart fails to pump adequate blood up to the brain. Strokes—often associated with high blood pressure—and senile "wearing out" of the brain also affect old people. Other common causes of brain damage are serious head injury (for example, in car accidents), birth disorders, and poisons such as excessive alcohol or carbon monoxide.

The aged person is frequently best cared for at home amid familiar surroundings. Drugs sometimes decrease anxiety, relieve depressions, calm and help reduce suspiciousness. Nursing home care is often needed.

Another group of disorders have the long name of *psycho-physiologic illness*. These are disorders in which it is felt that the mind (psyche) may greatly influence or perhaps even cause physical illness. Some of the diseases which may be affected to a large degree by emotions are asthma, obesity, rheumatoid arthritis, stomach ulcers, allergies, migraine headaches, and thyroid disease. Generally, patients with these disorders are cared for by nonpsychiatric physicians.

Normal people may become *temporarily* upset and emotionally unbalanced in times of stress. An adult, for example, may develop symptoms such as low morale, fatigue, abuse of alcohol, or anxiety following great stress, such as moving to an unfamiliar country, losing a job, or being bullied by associates.

Infants under stress may react by becoming apathetic or excitable or by having feeding or sleeping difficulties. Children under stress may temporarily develop habits such as nail biting or bed wetting or become behavior problems in the home, school, or community.

These temporary upsets will clear up when the stressful situation is changed for the better. The important concept of crisis intervention— which is discussed under "preventive psychiatry" —is applicable to help people endure and deal with stressful situations. By modifying a crisis at its beginning a person may be spared the anguish of a possible mental illness. The helping person tries to prevent mental illness by acting to tilt the balance of forces favorably in the patient and in the environment.

Treatment of mental illness may be divided

into two categories, psychological (including behavioral and environmental) and physical.

Psychological Treatment:

Psychoanalysis is a lengthy treatment procedure (sometimes lasting several years) applicable only to a few select patients, such as neurotics and some with personality disorders. Psychoanalysis is an ambitious form of therapy through which a patient may come to understand why he thinks and acts the way he does, enabling him to change aspects of his personality. The analyst clarifies and explains the patient's uncensored thoughts, wishes, and feelings. The patient lies on a couch. It should be mentioned that not all psychiatrists are psychoanalysts. Psychoanalysts undergo specific training after regular psychiatric training.

Dynamic psychotherapy is a crucial and common method of treatment. It usually involves seeing a patient one, two, or three hours a week for several months or years. Intensive dynamic psychotherapy may be accomplished in a short period of time. The therapist forms a relationship with the patient and discusses the patient's thoughts, feelings, and behavior. He explains what is causing conflicts within the patient and may or may not delve deeply into the childhood roots of the conflict. The therapist helps the patient to observe himself as clearly as possible, so that he will understand himself better. The patient speaks; the therapist clarifies and explains. Each therapist has his own approach toward achieving this goal. This type of therapy is well suited for the treatment of neurotics.

Supportive psychotherapy involves the use by the therapist of suggestion, advice, urging, and persuasive alteration of the patient's environment. It is an across-the-board type of treatment utilized especially when support of mental defense mechanisms is deemed important.

Group psychotherapy may use dynamic or supportive principles. Groups usually have about ten members with the professional acting as group leader (there may also be a coleader). Each individual forms relationships within the group. The group discusses feelings, thoughts, and behaviors of individuals and the group as a whole. Group therapy is used with patients with various mental disorders and seems to hold hope for treating alcoholics and others with personality disorders.

Milieu therapy is often used in a hospital setting. The aim is for the entire environment to be beneficial to the patient. Thus, the atmosphere and programs of the hospital are carefully developed. The therapist-patient relationship is but a part of the total program. The patient benefits from a team approach in which the physician, nurse, social worker, psychiatrist, occupational and recreational therapist, and others help the patient to help himself in a consistent way.

19

Behavior therapy focuses on current problems and behavior patterns. A person's past experiences and mental conflicts are not given prime importance. This type of therapy involves many different techniques which aim at fostering desired behavior and eliminating undesired behavior. In one type, for example, a person with a phobia may be taught to relax completely. In gradual steps he will then be exposed to the feared object until he no longer experiences anxiety in its presence.

Physical Treatment:

Drugs are widely used. Potent tranquilizing drugs such as Thorazine, Stelazine, and Mellaril have revolutionized the treatment of severe illnesses (e.g., the psychoses). They do not cure but help make recovery easier. Patients generally become manageable, more sociable, and less hostile with drugs. The drugs may also help to reduce suffering, suspiciousness, hallucinations, and other symptoms. It has been possible to care for many more patients outside the hospital since the tranquilizing drugs have been available.

Drugs have a less important place in the treatment of neuroses and personality disorders. The milder tranquilizers, such as Librium and Valium, help to reduce anxiety in some patients. Antidepressant drugs may be helpful in lifting depression although they tend to be slow-acting. A chemical called lithium may prove useful for the treatment of manic-depressive psychosis. Antabuse is a drug used in treating alcoholism. If a person takes Antabuse and then drinks alcohol, he will become violently sick with headache, vomiting, and weakness. The drug is successful only if the alcoholic can be induced to take it every day.

Electroshock therapy is a treatment in which a brief electrical current is painlessly applied to a patient's head. It is a safe, time-honored procedure of which the patient remembers nothing. It can be effective in treating severe depressions and is occasionally used in other illnesses. Electroshock therapy does not necessarily prevent recurrences of a mental disorder.

Critics of psychiatry have noted that some patients with mental disorders continue to see psychiatrists for many years. This is sometimes true, and these patients do not differ from individuals with certain physical illnesses, such as the diabetic who must take insulin daily and have periodic medical checkups, or from the patients whose acute flareups of medical illness are handled by the family physician. It should also be pointed out that a successful termination of one mental illness does not necessarily guarantee that the individual will not develop another one, any more than recovery from a heart attack protects a person from breaking a leg or having another heart attack.

2 Stresses of Everyday Life

Our bodies and minds function in a delicate equilibrium. Physically this fact is illustrated by the complex chemical and physiological mechanisms that serve to keep us breathing, eating, reproducing, etc. Mentally, it is illustrated by the equally complex mechanisms that enable us to love and to work meaningfully, to think rationally, to daydream, to appreciate beauty, and to conjure symbols which may serve to ward off unpleasant thoughts and feelings. A stress might be defined as a force or group of forces which unsettles this equilibrium. The force may be external (such as an auto accident or the death of a loved one) or internal (such as hardening of the arteries or the fear of leaving home). Some stresses are overwhelming for an individual and may produce a crisis. During a crisis a person may function in a disorganized way, experience anxiety and/or depression, be preoccupied with present problems and memories of past ones. The individual is hurting and is unusually receptive to help. Crises are usually of short duration as changes soon occur in the person himself and/or his environment. The individual will return to his previous state of equilibrium, establish a more adaptive one, or become maladaptive.

This chapter will briefly examine aspects of some of the common major stresses of everyday life and will discuss some ways of dealing with them. The purpose is to present in a developmental sequence some of the difficulties with which people often must cope.

The Childhood Fear of Leaving Mother:

All young children feel anxious and fearful at various times and with varying degrees of intensity. Anxiety may be generated by mental conflict, by frightening experiences, and through contact with anxious adults. Anxiety may be expressed as excitability, sleeplessness, poor appetite, temper tantrums, nightmares, diarrhea, nausea, fast breathing, and many other symptoms. One can readily observe a child who is closely dependent upon his mother becoming anxious when his mother leaves him or when a stranger approaches.

As children grow older, some anxiety is displaced onto objects—such as animals or darkness. The object selected may result from a real or imagined frightening experience. When fear of an object persists, the child may be experiencing a phobic reaction.

A common and troubling set of phobias may revolve around school. The first day of school may be anxiety-provoking. The child is not so much fearful of school as he is of separating from his mother and the security she represents.

Once in school a child is faced with proving himself, and will agree to compete or decide not to compete with his peers. His concerns may be transferred onto some aspect of school—perhaps a "disapproving" teacher or failure at some task or a bullying classmate—and the child may resolutely refuse to go to school. He may develop physical symptoms in order to avoid school. The idea of going to school is terrifying and he vehemently fights attempts to return him to the classroom.

A mother correctly may spend the first day or two in school to reassure her child that it is "safe" for him to leave her. Counseling for both child and mother is sometimes indicated.

Adolescence:

The period of adolescence has biological, social, and psychological facets. These maturational facets may be characterized by inconsistencies which are often associated with considerable stress for both adolescents and adults. For example, some adolescents reach biological maturity at one age, social and psychological maturity at another. Biologically, adolescence is the time of rapid physical growth and sexual development. Socially, adolescence is the time during which a youngster is preparing to assume adult roles, and is literally in transition between adulthood and childhood. He is expected to relate to the opposite sex in new and sometimes frightening ways. Psychologically, a youngster is attempting to emancipate himself from his parents while at the same time wanting desperately to remain dependent upon them and to retain their love. He tries to clarify and solidify his sexual orientation and to establish an individual identity.

As noted, a part of the adolescent is still very much a child and enjoys the comforts of dependency and parental control. The adolescent struggles, albeit ambivalently, against these dependent needs. He needs to rebel and to form groups with particular rules and principles and idiosyncrasies which command the utmost loyalty. Adults are excluded from these groups because the purpose of the group is to repudiate adult influence and to foster self-growth.

As adolescents mature, they will admit members of the opposite sex to their groups. Sexual attractiveness and accompanying fears of sexual inadequacy come to play important parts in the adolescent's life. Adolescents typically have great concerns and feelings of guilt around their own sexual fantasies. Those who are uninformed or misinformed about sex, who have possessive or unconcerned parents, who are placed in a repressive or seductive environment, or who have unresolved mental childhood conflicts may "act out," e.g., may run away from home, act promiscuously, or get into trouble with the law. "Acting out" implies that there are unconscious (as well as realistic and conscious) reasons for behaving and thinking in a certain way. All adolescents "act out" to a certain extent and for many reasons. Conversely some adolescents react to their sexual drives by temporarily renouncing sexual interests and by espousing intellectual concerns and ideals of purity.

As the adolescent moves into his post-high school years (age 17–22), he must make some important and difficult decisions about his future. Indeed, if emotional growth and development have lagged during "adolescent turmoil" years, many important problems may be almost impossible to resolve. The adolescent may not yet have "found himself." He may be in an "identity crisis." During this period he may complain that he is unable to relate to others, that he is dissatisfied with life, and feels depressed, apathetic, and preoccupied. He may experiment with drugs, with sex, with various jobs, social groups, and school courses. The college student may fail his examination or delay finishing his thesis. Among other factors, he is concerned about leaving the relative security of student status for the rights of the adult world.*

Group psychotherapy and sensitivity training groups (small groups whose members, under the guidance of a qualified teacher, intensely explore their feelings for brief periods of time) appear to be attractive to those searching for an identity; not only may their own perceptions be clarified, but also they may experience more clearly how others perceive them. Individual psychotherapy, both brief and long-term, may be indicated.

Marriage and Family Life:

People have multiple motivations for getting married. They include "true love," social pressures, a need to be independent of parental control, escape from an intolerable home situation, a supposed opportunity to "help" another person suffering from personal difficulties, and many others. Whatever the circumstances of family life, there is ample opportunity for stresses to develop.

The honeymoon may be an unhappy experience for a couple. If the couple has not shared

---

*To flashback a moment, this behavior may be related to "school phobia" and the fear of leaving the security of mother. In general, an anxiety-provoking situation in the present may reactivate the feelings connected with a somewhat similar, repressed (unconscious) earlier childhood situation.

previous sexual experience, the first intimacies may prove frustrating. The husband may feel sexually inadequate or may even be temporarily impotent; the wife may feel similarly inadequate with resulting anxiety and/or unresponsiveness. Homesickness, fatigue, and worry over making this "the happiest time of our lives" may contribute. Guilt or shame may produce psychological scars in immature partners that could color the relationship for some time after the honeymoon. Separations and divorces during the first year of marriage are not uncommon.

The reasons for divorce are as multiple as life experiences. Divorce may be a sign of psychological immaturity, an inability or unwillingness to work out problems; but it may also be a realistic, mature decision. It is sometimes stressful to one partner or to both, e.g., in the instance of a very dependent spouse. One encounters middle-aged women who have never held outside employment and who have made home their entire life. A divorce may bring on a severe depression. In fact, such depressions following divorce are common. A marriage "on the rebound" may alleviate symptoms, but may lead to future difficulties if the legitimate or neurotic needs of the couple are not mutually satisfied.

If small children are involved, a divorce is likely to be more stressful to all concerned. For example, a broken home may have some influence on emotional stability in later years. However, staying together to provide an unhappy home may be similarly detrimental. Thus divorce may be either helpful or harmful; each situation must be considered individually and uniquely.

Marital stresses commonly center around finances, sex, in-laws, and child rearing. The precursors of these stresses may frequently be found in the marital relationships of the couple's parents and/or in the relationships of the spouses to their parents.

Control of finances may signify dominance in the family. Difficulties arise when both partners desire positions of authority and cannot arrive at a workable financial compromise. The common sharing of money involves mutual trust, and it may turn out that marriage partners come to distrust each other. Poverty is a critical social stress.

Sexual stresses may result from ignorance and misconceptions about sex, differing sexual capacities, psychological conflicts, and reality issues (such as lack of privacy). Some people may be misled by the "marriage manual" approach and feel frustrated unless both partners experience orgasm at the same moment. Various aspects of impotence and frigidity may cause or result from feelings of anxiety, anger, fear, etc. Among other efforts, sex education at an early age—in the home and schools—may prevent stresses later on.

In-laws are the butt of many jokes and

mother-in-law trouble is an old cliché. In-laws can cause marital disharmony when they interfere with a couple's independence. The interference may be parent-motivated or couple-contrived. A wife who constantly turns to her mother for advice, for example, may fail to develop individual coping ability. In-laws may come between a couple. A stressful situation may arise when a person is "forced to choose" between his spouse and his family.

Worries about children can stress a marriage. A parent may become so involved with the children that the spouse is neglected. Arguments over discipline are common; the most common error is inconsistency—parents frequently behave and transmit and communicate in a contradictory fashion. Children may also become pawns. In a schismatic family there may be two secret or open warring camps. Parent is pitted against parent, forcing the children to take sides. In a skewed family, one partner tyrannically controls family life and may act as a parent to the spouse. Both schismatic and skewed families have been implicated in the fostering of some forms of mental illness in children. At times it may be tempting for parents to blame themselves (or to be blamed) for their child's behavior or emotional difficulty; or for a partner to blame himself (or to be blamed) for his spouse's mental illness. Accusations and blame are bound to be rash and guilt-inducing, and are to be avoided.

30

Finally, communication patterns among family members may create stress. One upsetting method is that of giving double messages; a member says one thing but indicates in nonverbal ways the opposite. A double bind occurs when a person is "damned if he does, and damned if he doesn't." In such a situation a person is seemingly presented with a choice of two actions, but in reality either choice will be a "wrong one." An example might be a wife who complains that her husband never pays her any attention; when her husband does pay her attention, she complains that he is meddling in her affairs.

Pregnancy and Childbirth:

Pregnancy is a physiological stress for every woman. For some, it also presents psychological stresses. Pregnancy may occur when one or neither partner is ready for it, e.g., when the partners are unmarried, when a marriage is on the verge of collapsing, when there are financial difficulties, or, perhaps most importantly, when there are psychological conflicts. Pregnancy may also precipitate hitherto latent psychological problems in the prospective mother and/or father. For some women pregnancy is a time of doubt, especially about the ability to be a good mother. Feelings of inadequacy and of anger at the unborn child are common. These stresses may be expressed through excessive vomiting and nausea, headaches, dizziness, fatigue, and the need

31

to be taken care of. Prenatal classes for expectant parents can be quite helpful in reducing fears. Psychotherapy may occasionally be necessary.

Under some circumstances a pregnant woman may seek an abortion, and in some instances it may be useful. In other instances, it is wise to counsel the woman to explore other alternatives. Recently, many states have been revising and liberalizing their laws so as to permit abortions under certain circumstances.

Methods of childbirth (twilight sleep, local anesthetic, spinal anesthetic, natural, etc.) vary, and each woman must decide the method she wants in consultation with her obstetrician. The same is true with breast feeding. For some women, natural childbirth and breast feeding are desired and may come easily. For others, the opposite holds true. It is possible for a woman to feel guilty about not (or not being able to provide) breast feeding or undergoing natural childbirth. Anxieties about the potential pain of delivery or about the possibility of producing a deformed or retarded child may interfere with enjoying the birth of a child.

As mentioned, the wife's pregnancy affects the husband too. During pregnancy and labor he may develop symptoms similar to those of his wife. He has to curtail sexual activities with his wife and prepare to share his wife's affections with the newborn child. He may also harbor doubts about his adequacy as a father.

32

Immediately after the birth of a child—the postpartum period—a woman may suffer "postpartum blues" or occasionally a severe depression and/or psychotic episode.

While the wife is hospitalized, in some instances a homemaker service might be contacted to help the rest of the family. A public health nurse may visit the home later on to aid the new mother, especially if there are physical or psychological problems. Some women are aided by having their mothers present in the home for a few weeks after the birth of the baby; others feel and perform better without them.

Working:

Selfishness, uncooperativeness, nastiness, and other immature traits may be tolerated at home and, to some degree, in school. At work, these traits usually cause difficulty. Employers expect cooperation and "an honest day's work for an honest day's wage." A person discontented at work because of emotional problems may manifest mainly physical symptoms; his employer may fire him or the employee may quit and move from job to job. Changing job situations may be stressful. "Promotion depression" is not uncommon. In this instance, a person may be so frightened of new and added responsibilities that he may either refuse a promotion or become depressed following a promotion.

The cause of "work problems" may be within

the individual (fears of failure, dependency issues, angry feelings, problems with authority, identity problems) and/or within the environment (hostile boss, poor working conditions). An exploration of intrapsychic, interactional, and environmental factors may be indicated.

Illness:

Illness is both unpleasant and frightening. Both the individual and his family suffer. Hospitalization is especially traumatic. For a family it may mean the loss of the breadwinner. For the patient it may signify the loss of his family. Mental health workers may be able to assist a hospital social worker who often initiates and then remains in contact with the family of a patient. She is in a position to aid the family during this difficult period and to help plan for discharge. She is a link between the hospital and the community, between the patient and his family.

Reactions to illness vary. As noted, fear is a common one—fear of dying or of "losing control." To be confined to bed is in itself a regressive phenomenon. The person is torn between his wish to be taken care of and his intentions to retain his independence and his dignity. In addition he is assaulted by strange people conducting strange examinations, which raise both anxiety and fantasy levels to unreasonable heights.

One of the harassed patient's most utilized defenses is denial; unquestionably, when appropriately employed it diminishes or erases some of the physical and psychological discomforts of especially serious and protracted illness. Of course, denial may go too far; it may, for example, keep a sick person from getting help.

Surgical procedures can be upsetting. They often stimulate fantasies around death and mutilation. Previously repressed concerns around parent-child relationships may be revived as a patient feels passive and helpless before the "powerful" surgeon and his knife. Surgery is followed by a sense of loss and sometimes by depression.

Specific surgery may present specific problems. Following eye surgery, for example, it has been noticed that some of those patients who had both eyes covered with bandages went through brief psychotic episodes. The abrupt cessation of light and color stimuli caused them to lose contact with reality.

In dealing with people who respond inappropriately to illness by denying its presence, it is necessary to slowly break through this denial by presenting the reality of the situation in a gradual manner. As a person comes to integrate reality he may slowly abandon the need for denial. The ill person may then be helped to express his emotions—which often are angry ones. Much anger may be really self-directed ("How could I let this happen to me?"), but it may be displaced onto family, friends, physician, or hospital. It is also important to help a sick person understand what is wrong with him; many have marked misconceptions about their illness.

Grief and Mourning:

The process of mourning is normal, important, and necessary for the mental health of the bereaved. It is a lonely, painful process. The work of grieving involves the gradual withdrawal of both positive and negative feelings associated with the dead person. The mourner may initially assume some of the characteristics of the deceased and intensely identify with him. He may feel guilty about previous thoughts or actions; he may feel depressed and fatigued, cry a lot, and experience many of the symptoms of a depression, but this is an appropriate reaction to a loss rather than a part of a maladaptive process. In time, the mourner overcomes his grief, anger, and guilt and returns to the activities of everyday life. If the work of mourning does not proceed or take place within a reasonable period of time (e.g., within a few weeks or months), the bereaved person may indeed go on to a severe depressive episode with relentless self-accusations and intense feelings of guilt. Or, he may "recover" and psychologically defend himself well, only to experience a depression at another time, triggered perhaps by another loss or, for example, the anniversary of a death. There are many internal and external factors which may interfere with or even postpone the mourning process. Sometimes, of course, the post-ponement is necessary; at other times the be-reaved should be encouraged to do his 'grief work.'

Aging:

As with adolescence, the process of aging has biological, psychological, and social aspects. Each aspect involves a change and for some people these changes may be quite stressful.

Biologically, women go through the meno-pause (approximate ages, 45–55) and no longer have menstrual cycles. Hormonal changes may lead to such symptoms as hot flashes and irrita-bility. Psychologically, a woman may experience feelings of inadequacy around her femininity and womanhood. A common misconception is that sex may no longer be enjoyable, and that her sex drive will decrease.

Men also experience a "change of life," which is often associated with job dissatisfactions and imminent or forced retirement (approximate ages 50–70). Definitive hormonal changes are less evi-dent than with women. Similarly, however, men undergoing these changes may mistakenly equate gradually decreasing potency with being unmas-culine and weak.

The most important external stresses for in-dividuals as they grow older include retirement, illness, death of a spouse or other relatives and friends, and children moving out of the home.

There may be a real or imagined loss of social position; a recognition that lifelong ambitions may never be realized; feelings of uselessness and fears of loneliness; apprehension concerning a real or imagined inability to compete successfully with peers and more especially with young people "on their way up" while an aging person feels "on his way down."

The most common responses to internal and external stresses are depression and to a lesser extent a paranoid feeling. These reactions are known as involutional reactions, and vary from mild disorders to severe ones with intense suicidal thoughts, guilt feelings, and agitation. In fact, sometimes electroshock treatment may be necessary.

In the elderly, an organic brain syndrome (explained in Chapter 1) may complicate the picture, may indeed enhance the psychological symptoms that have been brought on by numerous stresses. The older person adapts to these stresses (including organic deficits) in proportion to their quality and depth and according to his previous emotional capacities and personality makeup.

3 The Concept of
Community Mental Health

Mental health implies "the ability to hold a job, have a family, keep out of trouble with the law, and enjoy the usual opportunities for pleasure." (S. Ginsburg) Thus, mental health is necessary for a community to love, work, and play well. The principles for fostering mental health apply to all aspects of community life from law to architecture.

The ideals of community mental health are for individuals to develop and to apply knowledge that will (1) preserve and strengthen mental health and prevent mental disorders on a large scale; (2) detect and treat mentally ill people promptly; and (3) rehabilitate the mentally ill so that they can return to the community. These ideals aim towards comprehensive and continuous care for the individual and for the community. The whole community, its individuals and agencies, has a responsibility for emotional illness because the mentally disturbed person comes from a community, becomes ill in that community, should be treated in community facilities, and will return, it is hoped, to community life when he is well.

Social responsibility for fostering mental health rests with those who control community affairs and those in care-giving and educational positions, such as politicians, physicians, clergymen, teachers, and social workers.

The modern community mental health movement began when the high incidence of mental disorders encountered by the armed forces during World War II made clear the need to develop massive programs concerned with mental illness. Mental hospitals slowly underwent changes and the concept of the hospital as a "therapeutic community" became important. Rehabilitation programs for the mentally ill were established.

In 1949, the National Institute of Mental Health was founded. This was a great boost to the mental health cause as it meant that government leaders recognized the seriousness of the situation. NIMH was given power to dispense funds for mental health research and training.

In 1961, the Joint Commission on Mental Illness and Health gave its influential report on economic and manpower needs, research problems for massive mental health programs, and developments in patient care and community resources. In general, the report recognized that gigantic mental hospitals were not the answer and that more emphasis should be placed on the role of the community.

The Concept of Community Mental Health

The scene was set for President John F. Kennedy's historic speech on "Mental Illness and Mental Retardation," delivered to Congress in 1963. President Kennedy said:

> There are now about 800,000 such patients in this nation's institutions, 600,000 for mental illness and over 200,000 for mental retardation. Every year nearly 1,500,000 people receive treatment in institutions for the mentally ill and mentally retarded. Most of them are confined and compressed within an antiquated, vastly overcrowded, chain of custodial state institutions . . . .
>
> The time has come for a bold new approach. New medical, scientific, and social tools and insights are now available . . . .
>
> I propose a National Mental Health program to assist in the inauguration of a wholly new emphasis and approach to care for the mentally ill. This approach relies primarily upon the new knowledge and new drugs acquired and developed in recent years which make it possible for most of the mentally ill to be successfully and quickly treated in their own communities and returned to a useful place in society . . . .
>
> Such a new mental health program is comprehensive community care. Merely pouring Federal funds into a continuation of the outmoded type of institutional care

which now prevails would make little difference. We need a new type of health facility, one which will return mental care to the mainstream of American medicine, and at the same time upgrade mental health services . . . .

These centers will focus community resources and provide better community facilities for all aspects of mental health care. Prevention as well as treatment will be a major activity. Located in the patient's own environment and community, the center would make possible a better understanding of his needs, a more cordial atmosphere for his recovery, and a continuum of treatment. As his needs change, the patient could move without delay or difficulty to different services—from diagnosis to cure to rehabilitation—without need to transfer to different institutions located in different communities.

Following President Kennedy's speech, the Congress passed the Community Mental Health Centers Act of 1963. This provided for the appropriation of funds to finance partly the construction of nationwide community mental health centers. It also provided funds for research and treatment facilities for the mentally retarded.

By law, one Community Mental Health Center must serve an area containing between 75,000 and 200,000 people. Thus, several small communities may be served by one Center, while a large city may have several Centers. Everyone, without regard to age, social class, race or belief, must be given service. Of special concern to the Centers are the poor and the alienated, groups which heretofore have been out of the mainstream of psychiatric interests and services. The poor have a high rate of psychosis and of social problems, such as delinquency, truancy, crime, and marital disharmony. Communities with unstable family life, poor leadership, high rates of unemployment, and poor communication have correspondingly high rates of mental disorders. By remedying community ills, the mental health of a community improves.

A Center need not be a unit under one roof. Each community differs, and thus, its Mental Health Center should reflect the characteristics of that community. A Center must provide certain basic services, but may do so by utilizing many of the already existing community resources. A Center need not always build facilities. For example, a Center might work with an existing general hospital in establishing and operating a psychiatric clinic. In all cases, however, the local Center programs must fit into a statewide plan, for it is the state which administers the federal funds.

Each Center must provide the following

essential services: inpatient, outpatient, partial hospitalization, emergency, and education-consultation.

Inpatient services are especially aimed at short-term hospitalization, e.g., from one day to six weeks, though a few patients require up to several years. Immediate, intensive care is most beneficial to such emotionally ill persons as suicidal individuals, acutely ill psychotics, persons dangerous to themselves or others, confused elderly patients, alcoholics with delirium tremens, and children who have committed delinquent acts.

The goal of the inpatient service is to provide milieu therapy, intensive or supportive psychotherapy, and drugs or electroshock therapy as indicated, so that the patient can improve and then be transferred to another service in the Center program, such as outpatient or day care, or to a private physician. The hope is to reduce the need for long-term hospitalization. The inpatient service may be in a general community hospital and need not be part of a mental hospital.

Outpatient services represent the largest form of direct service by a Center, because the majority of mentally ill persons can be treated adequately as outpatients. The outpatient service is a vital link in the provision of continuous care. Centers attempt to locate outpatient clinics in readily accessible areas; this makes it easier for families to become involved. Another function of a clinic is to involve community agencies in mental health programs and to work closely with juvenile courts, family physicians, nursing homes, welfare groups, public health officials, family service agencies, school systems, and clergymen.

The Center outpatient service may differ from traditional psychiatric clinics in several ways: by seeing clients immediately and eliminating waiting lists, by allowing nonprofessionals, such as mental health workers, to assist clients, and by providing crisis intervention (see page 50).

Partial hospitalization services provide hospital care for a patient on a daytime, evening, or weekend basis rather than around-the-clock. Thus, some patients can stay home during the evening and come to the hospital for daytime treatment programs, or they may come to the hospital only on weekends. About one-half of the patients who were formally sent to mental hospitals can be treated adequately in partial hospitalization programs. These treatment programs may be the same as those in a regular mental hospital and consequently may be similarly staffed.

Emergency services provide twenty-four hour emergency care through a telephone service and access to the facilities of a hospital Emergency Room.

Education forms an important part of a Center's function. Educational programs are aimed at spreading mental health information to the community at large and to special groups, such as clergymen, physicians, health and welfare personnel, police, and school personnel. Good educational programs make the work of consultation easier and more effective.

Educational programs are directed toward (1) helping the community to realize that mental illness is not shameful; (2) developing community acceptance of and interest in mental health concepts; (3) helping people recognize mental illness; (4) encouraging people to seek help quickly when needed and informing them how to go about it; (5) enabling the community to understand and help the mentally ill; (6) promoting local treatment facilities, such as child guidance clinics and outpatient clinics; and (7) promoting programs to assure the spread of mental health concepts, such as classes in mental health throughout the school years or regularly scheduled discussions among fraternal groups.

Education may take place in a one-to-one relationship, such as a conference between a specialist and a public official or clergyman to explain the mental health concept and its programs; or it may take place in a larger setting, such as a meeting with a small group of legislators or public health nurses. It may be conducted in more formal lecture settings, such as a lecture to a PTA group or a group of physicians. Workshops and seminars are other educational settings which are frequently used.

Mass media acceptance of mental health goals is important for education and publicity. Newspapers, magazines, radio, and TV can be useful educational outlets. Articles and programs of an informational and/or documentary nature can do much to educate a community and promote a favorable climate for mental health programs.

Consultation: Mental health consultants work with caretakers (agencies, ministers, etc.), not with patients themselves. Consultation may be on a case basis or on a program basis.

In case consultation, the mental health consultant helps a consultee (usually of a profession other than that of the consultant) to improve his own mental health skills and to find the most effective way of handling a problem. At times, such as in the case of a multi-problem family, representatives from several concerned agencies may meet with a consultant to discuss a difficult case. Essentially, the consultant shares the burden of a problem; final responsibility rests with the consultee.

In program consultation, the mental health consultant gives advice to agencies, such as courts, schools, and civic groups, concerning the mental health aspects of their programs. He may be of help in setting up programs for recruitment, training, policy making, administration, and use of personnel. He may also be of help in solving problems within programs, such as factory absenteeism or poor police-community rapport.

A classic example of consultation is that offered to schools. The consultant may be invited in by a superintendent or principal because a group of teachers is having difficulties in dealing with disturbed children. The consultant might first acquaint himself with the school, its organization, personalities, and problems. He would clarify and define his consultative role. He might help the teachers to look at problems from different vantage points, might outline the possible causes of a child's problem, and would then help the teachers to formulate and carry out a plan of action that could help the child. By the provision of concern, support, and sustained interest in the teachers and in their problems, he may (indirectly) help to reduce their anxieties about working with difficult, disturbed children.

In addition to providing these six essential services, Community Mental Health Centers are expected to develop other programs. Diagnostic services may be offered to provide evaluation and recommendations for appropriate care. Rehabilitative services are needed to provide social and vocational rehabilitation. This includes prevocational testing, guidance counseling, and, sometimes, job placement. Pre-care and after-care programs are necessary for adequate preparatory and follow-up services for patients in hospitals, outpatient clinics, halfway houses, or foster homes. Training programs are essential for producing qualified mental health personnel. Research and evaluation programs enable a Center to define goals, to discover methods of reaching these goals, and to evaluate results.

The community mental health concept appears to fit most appropriately into a public health model, that is, the model of primary, secondary, and tertiary prevention. In the concept of primary prevention the person is not yet ill; in secondary prevention he is becoming ill, and in tertiary prevention we are dealing with a full-fledged illness. The task of primary preventive operations is to reduce the risk of becoming emotionally ill and to attempt to deter or prevent the incidence of mental illness via research, education, a focus on the mother-infant relationship, etc.

The task of secondary preventive operations involves early detection of incipient emotional illness, thus lowering the prevalence rate. As an example, crisis intervention during abnormal grief reactions may forestall pathological depressions.

Public health officials have had success in the early detection of disease. Tuberculosis is an example. Unfortunately, there are no simple chemical tests or X-rays that are helpful in detecting mental illness (with rare exceptions). The diagnosis of mental disorders is based primarily on the clinical judgment of the professional. Gross mental disorders can be detected, however, by a perceptive layman. Religious leaders and school teachers are in a particularly good position to detect early symptoms and signs of mental illness. In times of crisis many people turn to their clergyman first. Teachers are in day-to-day contact with children over a long period of time. The importance of early detection has been recognized by various organizations. The armed forces, for example, evaluate young men and women psychologically when they are inducted. Some colleges now screen entering students for possible mental illness.

The task of tertiary preventive operations is to minimize residual defects and impaired social functioning through the use of hospitalization and vocational rehabilitation.

The essential elements of preventive services are (besides consultation and education) research and crisis intervention therapy. Research is the cornerstone of prevention. Research projects are at the forefront of every good community mental health program. By supplying accurate information and new ideas, mental health workers are important to the success of research.

Crisis Intervention: Both mentally ill and "normal" people go through stressful times, such as death in the family, loss of a job, surgery, and change of location. For some people the stress may lead to an acute psychological disturbance; they are in crisis. A crisis is a temporary, emotionally distressing state, related to a variety of everyday situations, such as death, illness, marriage, sexual experience, job, and school problems.

A person first attempts to handle stress in his customary way. If this fails, tension grows greater, and he must find new ways of looking at his problems and new methods of solving them. If he cannot do this, he may develop symptoms, such as fatigue, despair, or excessive drinking. Eventually he may become mentally ill.

Crisis periods usually have clear-cut beginnings, such as divorce or death of a loved one. Periods of crisis are usually short—from a day to six weeks; therefore, action must be speedy to help mobilize inner resources and alter outer stresses. Crises may involve people other than the person under major stress.

People in crisis are usually easy to work with because great anxiety and social pressures make them feel helpless and dependent. Intervention at the proper moment can yield maximum results with minimal efforts.

If a person handles a crisis well, this may be a turning point toward mental health because he may learn techniques to overcome future crises. If a person handles a crisis poorly, he may handle future crises in the same way.

Many mental health centers are establishing crisis intervention clinics where troubled people can receive help immediately. Generally, psychiatric clinics have waiting lists, and therapy is geared towards fifty-minute sessions. Crisis intervention clinics, however, do not keep waiting lists and therapy sessions may be brief. The client may be seen daily for a week or two until the crisis period has passed. The therapist may be a psychiatrist, psychologist, social worker, or nurse. Conceivably a well-trained mental health worker may become a "crisis intervener."

Crisis intervention is an active process. It involves clear definition of the sources of anxiety, communication among the people involved in the stressful situation, and practical actions to help the person in crisis master his problem. Intervention is often aimed at changing forces in the environment. An example might be speaking with the employer of a client whose main stresses are related to work.

The sources of anxiety, for crisis intervention purposes, lie in the individual's present life situation. Investigation need not delve deeply into the past. Treatment is aimed mostly at conscious factors.

These cases are illustrative of crisis intervention. A young lady walked into a crisis clinic. She was very anxious and fidgety. Her husband had just received a draft notice, and she was frightened that she would soon be alone. They had been married only two months. The young lady had eaten very little for several days and had been having nightmares. She felt relieved to talk to a mental health worker. They discussed alternatives to her being alone—such as going to live with her in-laws since she did not get along well with her parents. As a result of three subsequent sessions a decision was made that she stay with her husband where he was to be stationed. The young lady also talked about her sexual "hang-ups." The mental health worker listened sympathetically. After consultation with the clinic psychiatrist, the mental health worker recommended to the lady that she might eventually wish to see a professional for psychotherapy. Her extreme anxiety about separation from her husband and her sexual problems were indicative of a neurotic disorder.

A man walked into a crisis clinic with tears in his eyes. He said he was thoroughly frustrated. His life had been going smoothly until one month ago when his two children were hit by an automobile. The hospital bills were piling up, and he was frightened at the thought of going into debt. His wife had accused him of permitting the children to play in the street without watching them closely. She spent most of her time at the hospital and reminded him of his negligence whenever they talked. She refused to sleep in the same room with him. He felt very bad and was extremely nervous at work. His office boss told him that he might lose his job if he didn't "straighten up." His boss said he was willing to help in any way. The mental health worker and a social worker brought husband and wife together for several sessions in which the wife vented her hostility. The boss was contacted, and he arranged for an extra week's vacation for the man and also recommended to the company credit union that a low-interest loan be given. The children recovered rapidly and soon left the hospital. The family situation settled down.

4 The Interview

This chapter will deal primarily with the telephone interview, but many of the principles can be applied to face-to-face interviewing. In order to learn how to interview well, you ought to observe professionals while they interview, take part in mock interviews, and review tape recordings of your own actual interviews. An outline of the chapter follows:

Before the Interview:

   I. *Purpose.*
      What is your purpose in interviewing a caller?
  II. *Expectations.*
      What does the caller expect of you? Do you have realistic expectations about your position?
 III. *Forms.*
      Be absolutely familiar with the form you are required to fill out and be accurate in recording information.

The Interview:

I. *Identify yourself clearly.*

II. *Concern.*

Give your constant attention to the caller and express your interest and concern in him personally.

III. *Identification of caller.*

Obtain the caller's name and find out where he can be reached.

IV. *Present problem.*

Get a short, orderly summary of the present situation and what set it off. Determine if you can be of help.

V. *Restatement.*

Frequently restate the problem to the caller in your own words.

VI. *Past problems.*

Briefly discuss the caller's patterns of behavior and the ways he handled past problems.

VII. *Inquiries.*

Form a general overview of the situation and be prepared to inquire specifically about serious symptoms. Suspect suicidal thoughts in depressed, desperate, or psychotic callers. Remain calm; assess the immediacy of the problem; make a psychiatric referral. Attempt to recognize gross symptoms of mental illness, such as delusions, hallucinations, or illogical thinking. Know where to refer callers with these and other problems.

VIII. *Personal and community resources.*
Find out the names of people whom the caller trusts and other agencies with which he is involved. Be familiar with local facilities.

IX. *Disposition.*
Discuss your recommendations with the caller. Make sure the disposition is realistic and acceptable to all concerned parties.

End of Interview:

Be encouraging. State your availability for further assistance.

Before the Interview:

Purpose: First of all, you must know the purpose of the interview. Are you gathering information only, or are you to be prepared to give answers also? If you are supposed to help the caller solve problems, then you must be prepared to get more involved than if you are simply collecting information.

Expectations: Try to put yourself in the caller's position. Why is he calling? What does he really expect? Are his expectations realistic? Can they be met? Are you familiar enough with your community to be sensitive to the different kinds of expectations of people of various racial, economic, and educational groups? What about your own expectations? An examination of your motives for being a mental health worker may help clarify your position. For example, do you really expect to make a difference in the caller's life, or simply to alleviate your own boredom? Your expectations should be expressed openly in group discussions with your coworkers and supervisors. Understanding your own motivation and expectations will help you in performing your job.

Forms: You must be absolutely familiar with the forms you are expected to complete regarding the interview. The form itself may also serve as a guide to you in obtaining information. It is usually best to write down information during the interview on a large pad and transfer it immediately after the call onto the official forms. It often seems like a waste of time and energy transcribing information, but this is just as important as the actual interview. In fact, no interview can be considered complete unless all the pertinent information is written down accurately in a way that others can utilize. Official forms may be aggravating, but they are necessary for proper evaluation and research, and also aid efforts to help the caller should you not be present the next time he calls. Forms make it easier for everyone concerned to find information quickly.

The Interview:

Identification: Be sure to identify clearly the agency and/or yourself at the onset and then follow with a phrase such as, "May I help you?" Forced cheerfulness is out of place, as is initial pessimism. A courteous interest should suffice. Further questions may be open-ended ones, such as, "Won't you tell me about your problems?"

Concern: At all times you must show concern, no matter whether you are jittery, anxious, happy, or depressed. Should the entire interview come to naught, your concern may be enough to help the caller weather a storm. Concern is beneficial and may be of more importance than any actual advice given or action taken. Show your concern in ways that are comfortable for you. Interject phrases in the conversation such as, "We should try to find ways to solve this problem," or "I certainly am concerned about you and your problem," or "I understand."

Identification of Caller: Take the name of the caller and find out where he can be reached. If the caller identifies himself initially, there is no problem. But the caller may be wary; he may want to see what you have to offer before he lets you put his name on your list. Do not force the issue too hard at first. As you feel the caller is warming up, you might ask, "Is there any place where I can reach you and for whom shall I ask?"

You must respect the privacy of the caller and not become angry if he refuses to give his name. Make sure, in this case, that you give him your name and tell him when you can be reached.

Present Problem: The next thing is to find out as accurately as possible why he is calling and why he chose to call you instead of some other agency. Try to record his primary reason verbatim in one sentence. Sometimes callers are so wrapped up in their problem that they start in the middle instead of at the beginning. If this occurs, ask, "Why exactly did you call?" If he is vague, say, "I don't fully understand why you called." Without knowing the reason for the call, you may waste much time on extraneous details. Vagueness, however, may be part of the caller's style of life, and you must be patient and attempt to understand.

Ask yourself then—is he calling the right place? Can you be of help? Often clients have been shifted from agency to agency. Do not let someone talk for half an hour before you tell him that he has called the wrong place. If you think that you may possibly be able to help the caller, tell him so at the time. "It sounds like you've called the right place and we will do everything we can to help you."

At this point you share, with the agency, responsibility for helping the caller. You must be aware of the type of relationship your agency expects you to form with the caller. In general, you will want to be concerned but not emotionally involved.

You then want to get a clear narrative of the present situation. When did the person's trouble start? At this time, do not go back over details of ten years ago. Concern yourself only with the present situation. What set off the problem? In chronological order, determine significant, recent events. This should be neatly formulated into one or two paragraphs and should read like a rapidly developing story. The details of the present situation should be clearly ordered in your mind.

Restatement: It will be of great help to the caller if you frequently restate the problem in your own words. Your restating of the difficulty may clarify it for him and help him solve it. Throughout the entire interview, restate the situation frequently as it develops. Restatement often leads to clarification.

Past Problems: Then ask about the past problems of the caller. Are they related to the present problem? How did he handle his problems in the past? Can he trace the historical roots of his problem? Ordinarily, not too much time is spent on this part of the interview. Crises need immediate attention with emphasis on the present.

Inquiries: At this point, you might want to stop and formulate a general overview of the problem. Then you may proceed to ask questions pertinent to the case with certain goals in mind. You should attempt to find out if there is more to the problem than is apparent. You are not expected to diagnose a specific mental illness, but you ought to recognize gross mental illness and emergency situations. By listening to the caller and by asking pertinent questions, you may become aware of symptoms indicative of severe mental disorders.*

By asking "How are your spirits?" you may discover that the caller is depressed. A severely depressed person is difficult to interview because he gives a bare minimum of information, sighs, and may take several minutes just to say "yes" or "no." Severe depression requires professional treatment.

Delusional thinking (false beliefs) may be easy to identify if the delusions are obvious, such as a person's believing that he is God or that there is a communist plot against him. But delusions can also be rather subtle and convincing, especially when they contain a germ of truth. A delusional person may strongly believe, for example, that his wife is unfaithful, but the story may be based on bizarre elements such as secret signals or odors. Frequent subjects of delusional systems are mailmen, delivery men, teachers, physicians, political figures, and famous personalities. A question to elicit delusional thinking is, "Do you feel that people are against you or laughing behind your back?" Feelings of persecution and false be-

*The topic of suicide is discussed in the following chapter.

62

liefs about a specific person may sometimes lead to future violence. All delusional callers should be referred for professional evaluation.

Bizarre language, hallucinations, illogical thinking, and strange feelings may indicate serious mental disorders. Such callers are in need of psychiatric help.

Personal and Community Resources: In deciding upon the best way to help the caller, you must know all the resources in your community in addition to the particular resources of the individual.

In times of emergency you should generally turn to the family first as a resource. There is usually at least one family member whom the caller trusts. If this is not appropriate, then ask the caller, "Is there anyone you especially trust?" If, during the interview, the caller mentions a family physician, clergyman, a special friend, a lawyer, or a community agency, be sure to record the name. In all cases be especially sure to ask about any community agencies that might be involved. The caller may not be satisfied with the agency with which he is involved, but you ought to know about it.

Disposition: In times of crisis an individual needs to be helped quickly. His enthusiasm for seeking help may be dampened by inappropriate referrals and by having to go from one agency to another before he reaches the one that meets his needs. If you are not absolutely sure what to tell a caller, arrange to call him back. Be honest; tell him you think you can be of assistance, but that you want to discuss the best solution with some other staff members.

Before making any disposition, ask the caller if he has thought of any possible solutions. Often, he will make the call with a solution in mind. You might also tentatively offer a few solutions and measure the caller's response. He may, for example, be unwilling to see a psychiatrist but willing to visit a family service agency.

In general, try to encourage the caller to stay with the agency with which he is already involved. If he is dissatisfied with the agency, then you might be in a position to get him and the agency together on a sound footing. You will be surprised at how often you can solve problems just by opening up lines of communication, bringing complaints out into the open, and helping people to understand each other better. Working with several agencies concerned about the same individual can be a touchy matter. Interagency competition and rivalries may hamper effective coordination of services. Professional advice is helpful before undertaking such a task. When referring someone to another agency, a mental health worker should obtain permission to divulge any information about him.

Do not make promises you cannot keep. For example, if your supervisor agrees with you that hospitalization is in order, do not tell a caller he can go to a mental hospital and be admitted there until you have contacted the hospital and made the proper arrangements.

You should not make a unilateral decision. Present your recommendation to the caller—if he accepts it, then you should see if the solution is workable as far as the other people involved in the case are concerned. If everything can be worked out, then call him back and give him the proper names and numbers to contact. Unless he is unable to, he ought to take the initiative. If the caller rejects what you consider to be the wisest decision, then try to help him understand why you think your solution is best. Should he still refuse, then help him work out alternative solutions.

End of Interview: Try to end your interviews on a slightly cheerful note. Do not be overly sweet or overly optimistic. Be as encouraging and as hopeful as the situation realistically merits. Remind the caller that you are concerned and available should he need further assistance.

At the Washtenaw County Community Mental Health Center, mental health workers frequently interview individuals asking for help. A record must be made for each contact. Dr. Lenin Baler, Director of Research and Training at the Center, devised the following form. Not only does it provide information about the contact, but it is also designed so that each item can be coded onto a computer card for research. The

research projects help to evaluate current programs, gather data for program planning, and
test hypotheses regarding the causes of mental
illness. The mental health workers attend several
conferences so that they understand the research
projects and learn the proper method of filling out
the contact forms. Thus, by providing services
and participating in research projects, mental
health workers are active members of the Center
team. Pages 67–74 constitute the "long" form.
Pages 75–76 make up the "short" form. Both the
long and short forms serve as official Center rec-
ords as well as research documents. Every contact
thus plays a part in the Center's research and
evaluation programs. For some projects the long
form is used, and for other projects the short form
is used.

Initial Contact Form
Part I — Face Sheet

_____
(Name of Primary Client)

_____
(Name of Secondary Client, If Any)

(8-11) Record Number

(12) Source of Contact	(13-18) Date of Call _____
1=Telephone	mo. day yr.
2=Walk-in	(19) Time of Call-Circle: 1=a.m. 2=p.m.
3=Mail	
4=Field Contact	(20-23) Hour of Call _____
9=Other _____	
(Specify)	(24-26) Duration of Call in Minutes _____

(27-28) First Center Staff Member	(29-30) How the person calling has
Contacted:	heard about the Center?
1=Mental Health Worker	1=Telephone Listing
2=Social Worker	2=Newspaper
3=Psychologist	3=Friends, Relatives
4=Psychiatrist	4=Community Agency
5=Nurse	9=Other _____
6=Education Specialist	(Specify)
7=Trainee _____	y=Undetermined
(Specify)	
9=Other _____	
(Specify)	

(31-32)   Who Has Called=(Primary Client)
    1=Self
    2=Parent
    3=Other relatives or friends
    4=Welfare or social service
    5=Educational agency
    6=Correctional agency
    7=Clergy
    8=(non-mental) health profession-
       al in private practice
    9=(non-mental) health profession-
       al agency
    10=mental health professional in
       private practice
    11=mental health professional
       agency
    99=Other_____
          (Specify)

(33-34)   Purpose of Contract
    1=Public relations
    2=Education (e.g. request for
      guest speaker)
    3=In-service training (e.g. request for
      a series of seminars for caretaker
      group)
    4=Request to participate in com-
      munity planning function
    5=Information request
    6=Request for consultation
    7=Client intake (i.e. a client be-
      comes the responsibility of the
      Center for evaluation, treat-
      ment, referral, etc.)
    9=Other _____
          (Specify

*Please state details of the contract on the attached Narrative Page.

Signed: _____
(Center of Staff Member First Contacted)

Initial Contact Form
Part II — Narrative Sheet

(8-11)
Record Number

A   Who has called=(Primary Client)

Name:_____

Agency Affiliation (if any):

_____

Address: _____

City: _____County: _____

State: _____Tel.: _____

B   Secondary Client (if any)

Name: _____

Address: _____

City:_____County: _____

State:_____Tel.: _____

C   Describe the Nature of the Request:

_____

_____

_____

_____

_____

_____

_____

_____

_____

_____

_____

_____

_____

_____

_____

_____

D   Initial Plans for Handling Request:

_____

_____

_____

Subsequent Contact Form
Part I — Face Sheet

_____
(Name of Primary Client)

(Please record in sequence every contact
with a client, referral source, and disposition
referral)

_____
(Name of Secondary Client, if any)

(8-11)
Record Number [   ]

1. Date of contact: _____ Time: _____

   Person contacted: _____

   By whom: _____

   Result of contact: _____

   _____

2. Date of contact: _____ Time: _____

   Person contacted: _____

   By whom: _____

   Result of contact: _____

3. Date of contact: _____ Time: _____

   Person contacted: _____

   By whom: _____

   Result of contact: _____

4. Date of contact: _____ Time: _____

   Person contacted: _____

   By whom: _____

   Result of contact: _____

5. Date of contact: _____ Time: _____

   Person contacted: _____

   By whom: _____

   Result of contact: _____

   _____

   _____

69

Please use this page to describe the salient details of the sequence of contacts and the outcome.

Case Record Form

_____

(Name of Primary Client)

_____

(Name of Secondary Client, if any)

(8-11) Record Number	

Classification according to major area of social malfunctioning.

(51-52)   Is this a family adjustment problem?
        1=No
        2=Yes, marital
        3=Yes, child training or management
        4=Yes, other: specify _____
(53-54)   Is this a school adjustment problem?
        1=No
        2=Yes, academic achievement
        3=Yes, school behavior problems
        4=Yes, other: specify _____
(55-56)   Is this a work adjustment problem?
        1=No
        2=Yes, achievement problem (e.g. promotion)
        3=Yes, work stress
        4=Yes, other: specify _____
(57-58)   If there is an area of social malfunction not adequately covered by those itemized
        above, please specify here: _____

_____

(59-70)   Classification of presenting problem according to major symptom or complaint.
        Please circle the one or the fewest number of symptoms or complaints most
        salient in the presenting problem.

        1=Financial
        2=Physical health problem
        3=Intellectual capacity or adequacy (excluding mental retardation)
        4=Mental retardation
        5=Sexual problems-Heterosexual
        6=Sexual problems-Homosexual
        7=Sexual problems-Other, specify _____
        8=Aggressive behavior or assaultive
        9=Suicidal tendencies
        10=Mood problem—anxiety, fear, panic
        11=Mood problem—depression, apathy
        12=Mood problem—guilt
        13=Mood problem—Other, specify _____
        14=Cognitive disturbance (disturbance of thought or memory, delusions, hallucina-
            tions, etc.)
        15=Self-adequacy or self-acceptance problem
        16=Addictive behavior—alcohol
        17=Addictive behavior—drugs other than alcohol, specify _____
        18=Addictive behavior—Other, specify _____
        19=Delinquency or criminal behavior
        20=Salient symptom or complaint other than above, specify _____

71

Classification according to chronicity of problem

(71)   Has this person ever received professional help for a mental health problem before?
0=No
1=Yes, psychiatric hospitalization—specify where and when _____

_____

2=Yes, other help—specify where and when _____

_____

y=Undetermined

(72)   Has the Washtenaw County Mental Health Center ever handled this person before?
0=No   1=Yes

(73)   Is the present problem a recurrence of the same or similar problem this person has
had in the past.
0=No   1=Yes   y=Undetermined

(74-75) Duration of present problem(s)
1=1-6 days
2=7-20 days
3=21 days-6 weeks
4=7 weeks-6 months, specify to nearest week or month _____
5=7 months-one year
6=more than one year but not life-long duration
7=life-long duration

(76-77) Please check any event below that occurred in this person's life situation in the
last six months.
0=None   8=Birth of a child
1=Physical illness   9=Menopause
3=Mental Illness   10=Upsetting sexual episode
4=Divorce   11=School failure or problem
4=Separation   12=Change of job or job problem
5=Death   13=Residential move
6=Marriage   14=Financial crisis
7=Pregnancy   99=Other, specify _____
                                    y=Undetermined

72

Case Record Form   (8-11)
                 Record Number

(12)   Do you see this case as a "psychiatric emergency"?
         0=No
         1=Yes, specify *your* reasons: _____

_____

_____

         y=Undetermined or unable to make a judgment

(13)   Do you see this case as a "crisis case"?
         0=No
         1=Yes, specify *your* reasons: _____

_____

_____

         y=Undetermined or unable to make a judgment

Disposition of the case.

(14)   Do you feel that crisis intervention was specifically provided during the Center contact with this case?
         0=No
         1=Yes
         y=Undetermined or unable to make a judgment
         If no referral was made in this case please specify why not _____

_____

(15)   If a referral was made in this case please specify:

(16-17) To whom (final referral only) _____

_____

(18)   Relative ease or difficulty in referral efforts _____

_____

(19)   Relative appropriateness of the final referral from the Center Staff Member's point of view _____

_____

(20)   Relative appropriateness of the final referral from the viewpoint of the person who is the case _____

_____

73

Social and Demographic Case Data

		(8-11) Record Number	

| (21-22) | (leave blank) Census Tract Number | (23-24) | Age in Years to last Birthday | (25) | Sex

1=Male
2=Female |

| (26-27) | Race
1=Caucasian
2=Negro
3=Other _____
(Specify)
y=Undetermined | (28-29) | Education—
Indicate Num-
ber of Years
Completed

y=Undetermined | (30) | Church or Religious
Affiliation
1=Protestant
2=Catholic
3=Hebrew
4=Other _____
(Specify)
y=Undetermined |

(31-32)   Occupation Status

1=Not in labor force-child   6=Working full time
2=Not in labor force-college student   7=On welfare or other type of assistance
3=Not in labor force-housewife   8=other _____
4=Not in labor force-retired   (specify)
5=Working part-time   y=Undetermined

| (33) | Marital Status
1=Single   4=Separated
2=Married   5=Common Law
3=Divorced   6=Widowed
           y=Undetermined | (34-35)
State the person's annual income
to the closest $1,000:

_____
y=Undetermined |
|---|---|

(36-37)   Living Arrangements

1=Living in family-male head of household
2=Living in family-female head of household
3=Living in family-wife of head
4=Living in family-child
5=Living in family-other relative
6=Not living in family-living alone
7=Not living in family-living in Rooming House or Hotel
8=Not living in family-living in military barracks
9=Not living in family-living in school or college dormitory or apartment
10=Not living in family-inmate of institution
11=Other, specify _____
y=Undetermined

| (38-39) | If the case is a dependent child or
wife, indicate the number of years
of education completed by
father or husband

x=not applicable
y=undetermined | (40-41) | If the case is a dependent child or
wife, indicate the total annual in-
come of the father or husband to
nearest $1,000.

x=not applicable
y=undetermined |
|---|---|---|---|

PERSONAL DATA
OUTPATIENT DATA SYSTEM

Facility Code & Name: _____

1. Case Number	2. Name (Last/First/Middle)	3. Type of Problem(s)*
5. Census Tract	6. Sex ☐1. Male ☐2. Female	7. Referral Date (Mo/Da/Yr)
8. Referral Source Code*	11. School Code: County	District School

13. Education: Number of Years Successfully Completed	14. School System Attended ☐01. Graded ☐02. Ungraded
16. Social Security Number (Suffix)	17. Date of Birth (Mo/Da/Yr) 18. Place of Birth (Code)

19. Marital Status
☐01. Never Married ☐02. Married ☐03. Separated
☐04. Widowed ☐05. Divorced ☐06. Widowed & Remarried
☐07. Divorced & Remarried ☐08. Unknown

20. Living Group
☐01. Alone ☐02. Spouse ☐03. Children ☐04. Parents ☐05. OtherRelatives
☐06. Friends ☐07. Foster Home ☐08. Institution ☐09. Unknown

21. Living Situation
☐01. Own Home ☐02. Rented Home ☐03. Rented Room/Apt. ☐04. Boarding Home
☐05. Hotel ☐06. Nursing Home ☐07. Contract Home ☐08. Family Care
☐09. Halfway House ☐10. Institution ☐11. Other ☐12. Unknown

22. Military Service ☐01. Yes ☐02. No ☐03. Unk.	23. Number of Dependents of Head of House	24. Profession & Code*
25. Current Occupation & Code*	26. Profession of Spouse & Code*	27. Current Occupation of Spouse & Code*
28. Gross Annual Family Income	29. Previous MI Hospitalization ☐01. Yes ☐02. No. ☐03. Unk.	30. Hospital Code
31. Type of Release*	32. Date of Release	33. Previous Service(s)*	34. Current Service(s)*

41. Vocational Training Program
☐01. None ☐02. Division of Vocational Rehabilitation
☐03. Michigan Employment Securities Commission ☐04. Other

42. Race — National Origin
☐Caucasian ☐ ☐1. Negro ☐2. Indian ☐3. Oriental ☐4. Mexican

43. Religion
☐0. Catholic ☐1. Jewish ☐2. Protestant ☐3. Other ☐4. None ☐5. Unknown

44. Remarks

* Indicates Codes

75

ON ALL ITEMS TO BE FILLED IN   "NA" for Not Applicable
(RATHER THAN CIRCLED) USE: "NK" for Not Known
   "NO" for None

TYPE OF RELEASE:

31 Withdrew	51 Convalescent Status	71 Escape
41 Family Care	61 Leave of Absence	81 Discharge

TYPE OF PROBLEM:

01.	Academic Underachievement	27. Occupational Maladjustment
02.	Agitated Depression	28. Phobias
03.	Alcoholism	29. Physical Complaints Related to, or
04.	Anxiety	Caused by Psychological Disturbances
05.	Bizarre Behavior	30. Poor Social Adjustment
06.	Compulsive Behavior	31. Problems Arising from Neurological
07.	Confusion	Impairment
08.	Cruelty	32. Reading
09.	Daydreaming	33. Retardation
10.	Defiance	34. Sexual Offenses
11.	Delusions	35. Sexual Problems
12.	Depression	36. Speech
13.	Drug Addiction	37. Stealing
14.	Eating Problems	38. Suicide Attempt
15.	Enuresis	39. Suicide Gesture
16.	Excessive Guilt Feelings	40. Suicide Thoughts
17.	Fatigue	41. Suspiciousness
18.	Fire Setting	42. Temper Tantrums
19.	Hallucinations	43. Thumbsucking
20.	Hyperactivity	44. Truancy
21.	Indecisiveness	45. Withdrawal
22.	Inferiority Feelings	46. Other Bladder or Bowel Control
23.	Marital Problems	Problems
24.	Masturbation	47. Other Antisocial Behavior Not Listed
25.	Nailbiting	48. Other Destructiveness Not Listed
26.	Obsessions	49. Other Agressive Behavior Not Listed
		50. Other Problems Not Listed

REFERRAL SOURCE, PREVIOUS SERVICE, CURRENT SERVICE, RELATIONSHIP:

01.	Alcoholics Anonymous	23. Self
02.	Boarding Care	24. Sibling(s)
03.	Children's Residential Treatment Center	25. Social Service Agency
04.	Clergy	26. Spouse
05.	(Deleted)	27. State Mental Hospital
06.	Day Care Center	28. Vocational Rehabilitation
07.	Employment Service	29. Other Health Agency
08.	Employer	30. Other Psychiatric Outpatient
09.	Foster Parent(s)	31. Other Psychological Service
10.	Friend(s)	32. Other Public Mental Hospital
11.	Guardian(s)	33. Other Relatives
12.	General Hospital	34. Other
13.	Local Health Department	35. Center for Forensic Psychiatry
14.	Nursing Home	36. Child Care Center
15.	Parent(s)	37. Court, Circuit
16.	Private Mental Hospital	38. Court, Probate
17.	Private Physician	39. Court, Recorders
18.	Private Psychiatrist	40. Day Training Center (MR)
19.	Private Psychologist	41. Marital Counselor
20.	Psychiatric General Hospital	42. Police Agency or Agent(s)
21.	School	43. Prison or Other Correctional Facility
22.	School for Retarded	44. Private Social Worker

OCCUPATION:

01.	Professional, Technical and Managerial	08. Structural Work
02.	Clerical and Sales	09. Miscellaneous
03.	Service Occupations	10. Student
04.	Farming, Fishing, Forestry (Laborers)	11. Unemployable Child
05.	Processing Occupations	12. Unemployable (Other)
06.	Machines, Trades	13. Unemployed
07.	Bench Work	14. Homemaker

5 Suicide

Through experience we have found that the topic of suicide is as frightening for a mental health worker as it is for a beginning professional. It is common to anticipate dramatic moments of being a hero by personally rescuing a life or of feeling guilty and disgraced for being a failure and having a person kill himself (ostensibly) because of your error. It may be comforting to know that mental health workers can overcome their anxiety about suicide and learn how to handle such problems well.

Your contacts with suicide will not be as dramatic as you might anticipate. About two percent of calls to mental health centers concern suicide, and only a very small number of people who seek help actually do kill themselves. The life and death of an individual is the professional's responsibility. Your responsibility is to advise the person concerned about suicide to seek professional help and to aid him in finding this help.

Why do people attempt suicide? Some suicidal persons will have a well-defined mental illness. People suffering from depression, especially those who are anxious and agitated, often have feelings of great guilt and worthlessness and may decide life isn't worth living. Some psychotics may commit suicide as a result of hallucinations and frightening delusions. Homosexuals and alcoholics often lack self-control and are also frequently depressed, either of which may make them suicidal. People with antisocial attitudes and aggressive tendencies may turn their aggression inward against themselves and contemplate suicide. Hysterical personality types are attracted by the "theatrical" appeal of suicide. Suicide is rare in the mentally retarded or in the manic person.

The majority of people who attempt suicide, however, are usually relatively "normal," at least up until the time of their impulsive action. Common stresses related to suicidal thoughts are death in the family, loss of a job, recent divorce or separation from a loved one, and severe physical illness. Young women attempt suicide frequently, but do not kill themselves very often. A suicidal threat by a man is generally a more serious matter. The older the man the more likely he is to succeed.

These points are illustrated in the following examples:

A twenty-one-year-old secretary who had just moved into a new city called a mental health worker. She said she was without friends and was very depressed. She was thinking of killing herself since she could not see any other way to end her predicament. The mental health worker listened sympathetically and expressed understanding of the caller's feelings. She informed her that help was available. The caller seemed to accept that there were alternatives to suicide and agreed to call a psychiatric clinic for an appointment. She did telephone and was seen two days later without incident. Emphasis in her treatment was on helping her to make friends and to socialize more.

The same day a woman called about her fifty-five-year-old husband. He had been depressed for over a month since losing his job. He had not slept for a week and would speak only about what a failure he was. He was now pacing the floor and had a gun on his dresser. The only person he seemed to trust was a son who lived 150 miles away. The mental health worker advised the woman to call his son immediately and ask him to come without delay. She was also advised to call the family physician and ask him to come to the house. She was to stay close by her husband until such help arrived. The son and physician persuaded him to accept hospitalization, and they accompanied him to a private psychiatric hospital where he was admitted immediately.

Most people who attempt or talk about suicide are asking for help. This may be the only method left for them to get sympathy and attention. If they can be convinced that someone cares about them and is willing to help them and that there is hope, they usually will not act on their suicidal thoughts. It is important, therefore, that you convey to a suicidal person the message that you do care, that you will help, that with professional assistance there is definite hope for the future, and that there are always alternatives to suicide.

Not many people say openly, "I am thinking of killing myself." They frequently will hint, however, in the hope that they will be prevented from going through with the act. Such hints may be through the use of words and statements, such as "desperate," "I'm at the end of my rope," "There's no hope left for me," "Nobody cares what happens to me," "I'm bored with life." When you detect such hints, ask the individual to explain himself more fully. Do not be afraid of implanting the thought of suicide in his mind. You might approach the problem by saying, "How does the future look to you?" If he replies grimly, then you might ask, "Have you been thinking of harming yourself or taking your life?" He may feel greatly relieved just to express this thought to you. If you can get an individual to talk about his suicidal thoughts, then he may eventually be convinced not to commit suicide and to resolve his problems in another way.

80

Here is an example of the way in which a person's suicidal thoughts were brought out into the open. A middle-aged woman approached a mental health worker. After twenty minutes the mental health worker was still unclear about the reason the woman was seeking help. As the conversation progressed the woman was still vague, but she made remarks about unfaithful husbands and unappreciative children. Gradually she spoke about feeling that she had come to the end of her line. No one cared for her anymore. She had lost her appetite for food and for living. The mental health worker asked her if she had any plans for the future. The woman began crying and did not answer. She was then asked if she had been thinking of harming herself. The woman breathed a sigh of relief and stated that she had been having such thoughts, but that she was a religious person and was embarrassed to talk about them. She then established a good rapport with the mental health worker and talked about her feelings. With the help of the mental health worker she made arrangements to see a psychiatrist the next week.

If you detect that a person appears acutely suicidal, see to it that he is not alone. The urgency of the situation is increased if the individual has a definite plan worked out and has a gun, sleeping pills, or other life-endangering objects available. Speak calmly and sympathetically. Find out if there is someone the person trusts. Get him to a hospital or possibly to a psychiatrist. A relative or friend may accompany him; you may need to call an ambulance or (occasionally) the police. You may need to make a home visit accompanied by the patient's physician, if possible. If the patient agrees to come for help by himself, advise him to take a taxi.

Many people thinking of suicide are still in relatively good control of themselves and may be referred to a private psychiatrist or to a mental health clinic. An attempt should be made to have them see a psychiatrist that very day or the next. You might ask such a person to call and check with you daily until he is evaluated.

Suicide prevention centers now exist in large cities throughout the nation. Professionals and mental health workers run these centers. A twenty-four-hour telephone service is usually available as a lifeline for disturbed people. This telephone service is a vital part of any such center and has the primary mission of attempting to convert suicidal emergencies into resolvable crises.

6 Alcoholism and Drug Abuse

Alcoholics and drug addicts are individuals who repeatedly use alcohol and drugs to such excess that their physical and mental health, social life, and economic abilities may be interfered with. Both groups of people have deep-seated personality disorders. They are often passive and dependent, come from broken homes, and are unable to combat anxiety, frustration, and loneliness through normal means. They rarely find satisfaction in work, nor do they form stable, mature relationships. While they childishly search for pleasure, their underlying mood frequently is one of depression.

The entire community suffers as a result of alcoholism and drug abuse. Industry is faced with lost work time, inefficiency, and industrial accidents. The highways are made unsafe. The police, courts, and jails spend much time in arrests, judgments, and punishment or "rehabilitation." Most tragic of all, however, are the difficulties faced by families of alcoholics and drug abusers. These families often lead desperate lives and need to utilize community resources.

When coming into contact with alcoholics, you ought to be aware that the alcoholic's family is often very much involved in his illness. Both the family and the alcoholic may be torn by conscious wishes to overcome the problem and unconscious wishes to continue it. The alcoholic, for example, may choose a wife who will coddle and nurse him like a mother. Some women are particularly suited to this task and prefer to have their husbands alcoholic. Some of these marriages may break up if the husband stops drinking because the wife may no longer feel needed.

Frequently it will be the family who contacts you for assistance. The alcoholic himself may be little motivated to seek help. He may deny that alcohol is a problem for him. He may be deceitful and manipulative in order to protect his liquor supply. His stated good intentions must be taken with skepticism on your part. Persistence and kindness ought to guide your approach.

You may be contacted for advice concerning an alcoholic who is frightened, shaky, restless, seeing things that do not exist, or feeling "bugs" on his skin. He may have the DT's (delirium tremens). This is a true medical emergency and such people should be taken *immediately* to a hospital.

Alcoholics Anonymous is probably the most widespread organization designed to help alcoholics, since it has chapters in almost every large community. A. A. is a group of rehabilitated alcoholics who meet frequently in local communities and offer support and guidance to alcoholics who ask for it. A person must come *voluntarily* to A. A. or he will not be admitted to the group. The only requirement for membership in A. A. is the desire to stop drinking.

A. A. stresses the spiritual road to recovery (the organization has been called a religious cult by some), but does not believe in ever "curing" an alcoholic completely. "The course of the disease may be arrested, but the alcoholic must fight a daily battle." The alcoholic must accept the fact that he can never drink again for "one drink is too many—twenty drinks not enough."

A. A. offers a lifetime follow-up for all members. Individuals are specifically assigned to support and guide one another. This intensive interest in and understanding of alcoholics (an alcoholic can hardly deceive or beguile a group of ex-alcoholics) makes the organization a fine resource for therapy. Alanon, a section of A. A., is an organization of families and friends of alcoholics who need help in coping with problems. Families can be members of Alanon even if the alcoholic member does not attend A. A.

Specific professional help for alcoholics is frequently needed. Often there will be professionals in your community who "specialize" in treating alcoholics, and you should have their names available for appropriate referral.

Social service agencies can be of help to families of alcoholics. The families may need counseling on economic matters, psychological support during crises, and actual psychological and casework treatment.

Requests for help, such as the following, are common. The wife of an alcoholic contacted a mental health worker and said she was desperate. Her husband had lost his job because of drinking. They were about to be evicted from their home. The mental health worker put the woman in contact with a Catholic Social Service Agency. There she received help rapidly in finding a way to remain in her home. She also spoke with a social worker and was able to regain some emotional equilibrium. Her husband was persuaded to attend A. A. He stopped drinking and found a job. After several months he stopped going to A. A. meetings and in three weeks began drinking again. He then started attending A. A. meetings again regularly. His wife participated in the A. A. program for wives of alcoholics. Having a better understanding of herself and of her husband, she was able to support him psychologically. At last contact he had not taken a drink in fifteen months and was very active in A. A. This case points out and illustrates the frequent necessity for multiple agency intervention.

Another problem you may be contacted about is drug abuse. Drug abusers are often like alcoholics in their personality structure. The problems they create for their families and for society frequently call for the attention of many community agencies. The requests of addicts need to be handled with caution; many are in difficulty with the law.

The most serious form of drug addiction is that to heroin and morphine, potent and narcotic drugs which are addicting after brief exposure to them. Heroin and morphine addicts live mainly in urban slum areas. Typically the user belongs to a street gang and is introduced or seduced to use the drug by fellow gang members. Since the drugs are illegal, they are costly, and the addict will probably turn to crime to obtain money.

Synanon is a relatively young organization to which you may refer motivated addicts. Physicians may refer addicts to special federal hospitals. Social service agencies often must help the entire family of an addict. Some large cities and states have public clinics and halfway houses for addicts.

Another problem is that of barbiturate abuse. Barbiturates, such as phenobarbital, Seconal, Nembutal, and Amytal, are commonly used as sleeping pills. They are relatively easy to obtain and are not expensive. These pills can cause confusion and lead to overdosage and accidental death. Professional evaluation of barbiturate abusers is indicated.

Amphetamines, such as Dexedrine and methedrine, are stimulants and currently play large roles in the drug-abuse scene. In small doses they are sometimes prescribed by physicians for such effects as decreasing appetite, combating fatigue, and (paradoxically) calming hyperactive children. Some thrill-seekers inject the drug in large doses and go through three- to five-day "runs," during which they go without food or sleep and often perform useless, repetitive acts. Sometimes amphetamines produce a psychosis similar to paranoid schizophrenia. With proper treatment—hospitalization is indicated—this form of psychosis may clear up in about ten days. "Speed kills" is an expression known to most drug-abusers; it refers to the fact that injected amphetamines ("speed") may lead to sudden death. Some drug abusers take amphetamines to feel "high" and then take barbiturates to "come down." A person caught in the vicious cycle of amphetamine-barbiturate abuse is in need of professional help.

Marijuana, a drug used by all strata of society, is fairly easy to obtain and in this country is smoked mainly for its effects. Some of its actions are like those of alcohol. It may cause hallucinations, loss of sense of time, heightened sensitivity to the environment, and disorientation. It rarely acts as a sexual stimulant. It may serve as a stepping-stone to the use of heroin and morphine.

By attempting to withdraw and to escape from reality, chronic users of marijuana signify that they cannot cope with life normally. This may be a symbol of defiance against social customs and authority figures, such as parents and professors. Some artistically inclined users claim that this drug and LSD help them in writing or painting, but this, in general, is not an accepted fact.

The college student or other individual of stable background who experiments several times with marijuana need not be of great concern, but there are many people with unhealthy emotional backgrounds who see marijuana as a "cure" for their own emptiness. In general, you should refer *habitual* users of marijuana to a professional for evaluation. Often counseling is enough, but psychotherapy may be indicated.

Users of LSD and other so-called "mind expanding" or psychedelic drugs are generally users of marijuana also. Most of the marijuana mystique surrounds these more potent and harmful drugs. Although there are slight differences in the effects of the more potent drugs, their users often experience visual hallucinations, feelings of power, loss of logical thinking, disorientation, loss of control, and "uniqueness" of the environment. These feelings have been praised highly by those who have had a "good trip." While under the influence of the drugs, users have been reported to leap out of windows because they thought they could fly, to walk unawares into dangerous situations, or even to commit murder. There are many users who have terrifying experiences while under the influence of these drugs—the so-called "bad trip."

Individuals who are most drawn to these potent drugs are often those whose psychological state should preclude their taking them. An emotionally disturbed person can literally be destroyed by these drugs. The state they induce can be like schizophrenia. Sometimes this schizophreniclike state remains permanently, or it may even appear several months after taking the drug.

It appears that most users stop taking these drugs after a few years. They "outgrow" them, perhaps because they have too many "bad trips," because they are disappointed that their minds, even when expanded, are not richly endowed, or because they become used to the drugs and no longer have unique experiences.

LSD is a dangerous drug. The status of marijuana is not yet definitely settled, although there are indications that it is not harmless. The legal restriction upon use of these drugs is aimed at protecting those who may be seriously harmed even though it prevents others from having "pleasant, though hardly essential experiences."

You may be faced with a case such as the following. A college dropout was brought to a mental health clinic by several friends. He was very frightened and felt that if anyone touched him he would disintegrate. His friends reported that he had taken LSD several hours earlier and was on a "bad trip." Since quitting school he had made a living by making candles and selling marijuana. His mother was a chronic schizophrenic and he was frightened that he might one day be like her. The mental health worker called the clinic psychiatrist and a potent tranquilizer was given. The young man soon felt calmer, and his friends took him home and agreed to spend the evening with him. The next day he came in for psychiatric evaluation and was thought to be a borderline schizophrenic. He was unwilling to give up drug experiences or to return to the community as a responsible citizen. He felt that drugs helped him to understand himself better and to achieve harmony and peace with the universe. He mistakenly thought the life he was leading would protect him from mental illness while in reality it was bringing him closer to it.

Modern treatments for users of "hard" drugs (heroin and morphine) center upon inducing the addict to accept medically prescribed substitute drugs that reduce the pleasurable effects of narcotics and make the problem more controllable. Group psychotherapy and counseling in regard to employment, living conditions, and social contacts are also important in the total rehabilitation of the addict. It is encouraging to note that many young addicts, for unknown reasons, may "kick the habit" when they reach middle age.

The abuse of marijuana, LSD, and other hallucinogenics has recently come into prominence, and the results of treatment for this problem are not well delineated. Individual psychotherapy appears to be the most common approach. Research into the different aspects of these drug problems is progressing. Until more is known about these drugs, especially the long-term consequences of their use, society's attitude towards them will probably remain controversial. Time will tell whether the abuse of these drugs is a fad or a persisting pattern.

7 Community Resources

One of the basic responsibilities evolving out of the community mental health thrust is the appropriate delivery of services. Presently, five percent of the population of the country receive about ninety-five percent of the mental health services. More people need these services and could make use of them. Services should be accessible, opportunity to obtain them available. The community mental health approach tends to direct services towards high-risk groups such as the alcoholic, the suicidal person, the aged, and the poor. The services may be organized according to the needs, wants, and particular resources and idiosyncrasies of a community. Each community agency delivers what it wants to and what it does best. A goal of the community mental health movement is to make maximum use of community resources by paying attention to community needs and wishes.

Mental health workers ought to be familiar with the mental health needs of their communities, with their agencies and resources, and with their care-givers. The primary agencies and individuals with which clients will come in contact fall into many categories and include: hospitals, clinics, private physicians, social service, psychological and psychiatric agencies, educational facilities, self-help organizations, legal-correctional facilities, the clergy, employment and humanitarian agencies. A mental health worker needs a working knowledge of these facilities and their programs.

This chapter will delineate and comment on several widespread resources, with the recognition that the list is incomplete and that local issues determine their relative importance within the community mental health framework.

Child Guidance Centers provide diagnostic, consultative, and outpatient treatment services to children. Family treatment is often provided. Some child guidance centers have day-care facilities. They are staffed by psychiatrists, psychologists, and social workers. In some instances their staffs may also include teachers, occupational therapists, and recreational therapists. They are often the best resources for referring children. Some state hospital and university facilities also have children's day-care programs and inpatient facilities.

Children with significant mental retardation can be placed in special state institutions. Sometimes the waiting lists are quite long, and there may be a delay of a year or more before the child is admitted. Community Associations for Retarded Children may have day-care centers. They provide education and discussion classes for parents and often supply a bus service for retarded children.

The adolescent is often too old for a child guidance clinic and too young for an adult outpatient clinic. He frequently upsets the community by his behavior. Communities, in general, have not provided adequately for the mental health care and treatment of adolescents, many of whom are referred to "training schools" or "detention homes." Residential treatment centers are not hospitals, but are rather institutions where "problem children" live and attend school in a therapeutic environment. Some universities and state hospitals have inpatient facilities for adolescents. Organizations, such as YMCA and church groups, may provide programs and counseling for adolescents. School social workers and counselors deal with multiple adolescent problems. Some police departments have developed active "big brother" programs to help teenagers.

Outpatient help is available through private professionals (mostly psychiatrists) and psychiatric clinics. Clinics are generally centers for diagnosis, referral, and treatment—individual and group psychotherapy, casework, and family therapy. Outpatient services often are the largest aspect of a comprehensive Community Mental Health program and also are an integral part of state hospital programs.

Social service agencies, such as Family Service, Catholic Social Services, and state departments of welfare, handle large numbers of people who have problems in living and mild emotional disturbances. Social workers in these agencies help individuals or families to adjust chiefly by delineation of their problems, casework, and personal counseling. The main problems encountered are marriage conflicts, difficulties with children, and general family disturbances. These agencies also frequently have child adoption and foster-care programs. Fees for services are often low.

Families with multiple problems are handled well by these agencies. In one family, for example, the agency helped the mother to receive medical care for a goiter, the father to get a job through the state employment bureau, an unmarried daughter to place her unwanted child for adoption so she could continue school, and a son to be evaluated at a child guidance clinic.

State welfare departments have numerous programs administered by social workers. Appropriate referrals include the indigent, the blind, the aged, and the disabled. With regard to the ADC (Aid to Dependent Children) program, financial aid is given for children who are deprived of parental support; they must be living in homes that meet certain health and care standards. The Protective Services Division typically concerns itself with problems of child abuse (physical harm) and child neglect (emotional harm).

Most states have a vocational rehabilitation program. In general, these programs provide the physically and mentally handicapped with counseling, on-the-job training, psychological testing, job placement, and help with emotional adjustment to situations. Sheltered workshops are places in the community where individuals can work at tasks within their ability without great pressure. Most sheltered workshops deal with the physically handicapped, but they are rapidly being established for mentally ill and retarded patients. Some programs pay employers for on-the-job training of patients. For example, a man called the crisis clinic about his twenty-three-year-old brain-damaged grandson. The grandson could perform simple tasks but had not had a job for several years. The family had formerly lived in another state, and he did not qualify for vocational rehabilitation there. The mental health worker contacted the local vocational rehabilitation office and discovered that the grandson could probably qualify now. He was evaluated, received training, and was placed in a job. His employer was paid by vocational rehabilitation to help him settle into the job.

Every state has state mental hospitals. These

are usually quite large, roughly averaging two thousand patients per hospital, and may serve a specified geographic area. Patients and families who can afford it are usually assessed reasonable fees. A person who becomes ill can be hospitalized in a state hospital even if he is not a resident of that state. Through state hospital policy he will later be returned to his own state hospital system.

Because of their size, state hospitals can accommodate a wide variety of patients. Often they are the only feasible places for long-term hospital care, though most have acute illness services as well. Most patients needing hospitalization will be admitted to the hospital upon presenting themselves. In the case of alcoholics, however, many state hospitals now require that they be legally committed if they wish to be hospitalized.

Because of limited budgets and historical accident many state hospitals are physically unattractive and are understaffed. Nevertheless, they have, in general, kept pace with advances in psychiatry and are not the frightening places that many think them to be. The modern policy of most state hospitals is to return the patient to the community as soon as possible.

Private psychiatric hospitals are usually expensive and provide many comforts for patients. Some require a substantial financial deposit before accepting a patient; some insurance programs are fortunately covering psychiatric hospitalization.

University hospital psychiatric units are dedicated to training mental health personnel and doing research. Therefore, patients may be carefully selected for admission.

Veterans Administration Hospitals are located throughout the country. Some provide long-term psychiatric care, others short-term care. If the veteran's illness is service-connected, he will be admitted without question. Admission policies for all veterans, however, are usually liberal.

Modern psychiatric literature emphasizes the need for *community* hospital facilities for the mentally ill. The longer a person is a patient in a distant hospital the more easily he may be forgotten by family and friends. The trend is for general hospitals to add psychiatric units, and for small psychiatric hospitals to be built locally.

Many mental hospitals, rather than providing custodial care, now attempt to make the entire hospital a "therapeutic community." Social and emotional deterioration of patients is being reversed and prevented by changes in the physical setup of the hospital and the attitudes of the staff. Some examples of improvements are: formation of patient clubs and governments; small financial rewards for patient initiative; more facilities for both privacy and group involvement; patient social events; patient contact with local civic groups; patient participation in extra-hospital community activities, such as church or the movies; bright colors and lighting; comfortable furniture; and even ward pets. The patient's dignity is maintained and enhanced by reducing many of the undesirable effects of hospitalization.

It is important to call a hospital first to find out its admission procedure and bed availability before advising a client to go there. If a person truly needs hospitalization at that very moment, financial, training, and research needs are usually set aside and the patient is admitted. He may later be transferred to a more appropriate hospital. Any patient who appears at the emergency room of a general or psychiatric hospital becomes the responsibility of that hospital. Emergency-room personnel will attempt to make an appropriate disposition. For example, a potentially homicidal, psychotic man was brought to the emergency room of a private mental hospital late at night. The patient could not afford long-term treatment there but needed immediate hospitalization. He was kept in the hospital that night, and plans were made the next day to transfer him to a state hospital.

Many hospitals now have after-care programs which provide psychological and social care for patients after discharge. Social workers and public health nurses in conjunction with local agencies keep in touch with patients and support them materially and psychologically for as long as necessary. They often visit patients at their homes. The goal is to make further hospitalization unnecessary if possible.

Many patients need some sort of transitional residence before returning to the community. Halfway houses suit this purpose very well. A halfway house is a small residence in the community. It often is a large old house and has a home-like atmosphere. It may have an individual name, such as "Gateways" or "Portals." It is a self-contained residence and its function is mainly to deal with the psycho-social problems of the patient—providing him with companionship, understanding, and support in a somewhat protective atmosphere. The halfway house may hire a "house mother" to "take care of the house." Professional workers help the patients with specific problems. Patients often work during the day in the community and then help pay for their own room and board. The usual stay is less than six months.

Foster homes also serve a transitional role. These are private homes that are screened, supervised, and subsidized by the agency responsible for the patients. Social workers and mental health workers continue to work with patients and meet with the foster family to provide guidance.

Partial hospitalization provides inpatient care on a part-time basis. Many patients work in the community during the day and return to the hospital at night (night hospital). Others return to the hospital only on weekends. Many take advantage of day-care units, returning to their own home in the evenings.

Family-planning programs may prevent the

conception of unwanted children. Unwanted pregnancies may cause distress to parents and society as well as to the child himself. Planned Parenthood Leagues are active in this field as well as in genetic counseling. Genetic counseling by physicians involves helping couples to decide on the desirability of having children when there is a possibility of passing on hereditary illness. Some aspects of mental retardation may be genetic in origin.

Proper prenatal care is important in helping to prevent premature and/or defective births. Many public health clinics and obstetricians provide classes for expectant parents to prepare them for childbirth so that they can know what to expect and how to handle problems.

Well Baby Clinics have been in existence for many years. Regular visits to a Well Baby Clinic or to a physician provide for an ongoing relationship between mother, child, and physician and a detailed chronological history permitting early detection of any disorder in the child. These clinics often offer classes in emotional development, giving parents a better understanding of how to deal with their children.

Day-care centers and nursery programs allow early socializing among children. Cooperative nurseries, in which mothers take turns working with professionals in caring for their children, provide good experience for both mothers and children. Some nurseries are set up especially for the day care of preschool children whose mothers must work to support the family.

Schools are important community resources and occupy a central part in any preventive program. The school can serve as a healthy environment in which to grow, learn, and socialize. The origins of mental illness are often found in childhood. Aggressive or compulsive behavior, blocks to learning, failure to conform to classroom regulations and rules, abrupt changes in behavior, crying, social isolation and withdrawal, sudden loss of interest in learning, excessive fears, and failure to develop verbal skills are all warning signs that teachers may detect and act upon. Schools usually have social workers, nurses, "counselors," or special teachers who work with the teacher, the child, and his parents. School facilities often include speech correction and special classes for the physically, intellectually, or emotionally "handicapped." Day-school centers for the trainable mentally retarded may be available. Some school systems have classes for pregnant girls which allow them to continue their education and to receive counseling and health services.

Of the community adult self-help groups, Alcoholics Anonymous is perhaps the most widely known. It is discussed in the chapter on Alcoholism.

Recovery, Incorporated is a self-help association of former mental patients and "nervous" people. At weekly meetings members learn to handle everyday frustrations and irritations. Mutual aid telephone calls (limited to five minutes a call) and specified reading material are stressed. The group aims to complement professional help for the mentally disturbed.

The mental health worker may be in contact with the courts and court social workers, with the police, and with legal aid clinics. These are important community resources.

Occasionally, involuntary commitment to a hospital is necessary. For example, a man came to a mental health clinic because his wife was hearing voices and was accusing him of trying to poison her. She refused to talk to anyone or to go to a hospital. She was psychotic (not in contact with reality and unable to think logically). The only way to get her to a hospital was to commit her. Her husband was sent by the mental health worker to a probate court judge to file a petition for commitment. Two court-appointed psychiatrists examined her and recommended commitment. She was then taken forcibly by her husband to the state hospital and admitted there through court order. Fortunately, she recovered rapidly and was discharged home in four months.

Policemen are often involved with mentally ill people, people in crisis, and individuals who attempt suicide, and they may be called upon to intervene in serious family quarrels. The police may help by providing emergency transportation for a mentally ill person or by accompanying mental health workers on a potentially hazardous home visit. Policemen in plain clothes and unmarked cars are preferable when dealing with a mentally ill person. Each community has to form its own program of cooperation between the police and mental health personnel.

Legal aid clinics provide legal advice and services for people who cannot afford to pay a lawyer. Criminal offenses are not handled. Most commonly, help is given for divorce cases, eviction proceedings, and other civil matters.

Finally, programs for the psychological care of the elderly are designed to maintain feelings of self-esteem. Developing alternatives to early retirement is a challenging concern. Senior Citizen Guilds and Community Center programs provide opportunities for making new friends and learning new skills. Entire communities for elderly people have met with mixed success as there are some who prefer to stay with, and do best in the company of, younger people.

8 Epilogue

We are impressed with the great number of people needed to establish comprehensive services, to deliver these services, and to implement a preventive orientation towards mental illness. How will we be able to staff our mental health facilities appropriately to do the job? The mental health worker seems to hold a key position. Besides meeting certain mental health manpower needs (e.g., suicide prevention and crisis intervention), the lay volunteer as a *citizen of her community* may serve certain roles and functions which are critical and necessary to the community's mental health. In addition, she is in a position to form a career pattern which will be helpful to her, her family, and her community.

The mental health worker can combine her inherent skills and common sense, her previous experience, training, and her newly acquired on-the-job knowledge to work productively for her community. She may become involved with her community's organization, development, and planning. She may act as an intervener, a facilitator, an expediter, and may participate in a wide range of comprehensive community mental health services. She will be close to people in need, and will know the helping resources of the community. She may become an important link in a health system that stresses continuity of care. Finally, and we believe most importantly, she will serve an advocacy role, as an *agent for social change* and a *participant in social action*. It is her attitude and orientation toward the "disadvantaged" of the community, toward the poverty stricken, socioculturally disorganized, high-risk groups that will set the tone, the intent, and the activity of the mental health facility of which she is a vital part.

The mental health worker is concerned primarily with the environment of the potential patient, and she insists that the community share responsibility for the welfare of its members. She is action- and service-oriented and emphasizes the social world outside of institutions. She is aware of and interested in certain subcultural groups in which an individual may act quite differently (and deviantly) from the standards of the larger culture. She understands and is able to deal with both cultures and acts in the interests of the "deviant." The mental health worker does not have (and should not have) the same illness-oriented approach which medical and other mental health professional training provides. As a part of a social system which requires change to survive, the mental health worker is in a better position than the professional to help effect change. As a link between the "establishment" and the rest of the community, she connects various social systems and relates to the customers and clientele of the systems.

As "walk-throughs" and "hand-holders," as enablers and facilitators, mental health workers increase access to services for those heretofore deprived of, or ignorant of, opportunities. Access is accomplished through a host of methods and means including education, forming relationships with other agencies, assistance in job hunting, and the like.

A basic responsibility of a mental health community is the appropriate delivery of services to appropriate people. Ideally services should be organized according to the needs, wants, particular properties, and idiosyncrasies of a community. Thus, services (and power) should be accessible to everyone, and the opportunity to obtain them available. People in need usually require an ally, an advocate who may attempt to survey and, indeed, to organize people to speak on their own behalf. The mental health worker can learn to be an advocate, learn how to go into an established community to obtain the services she desires, and learn how to control these services once they are obtained. This advocate function, with its crucial community linkages, may indeed be the most important role to be carried out by the "new professional," the mental health worker.

The "new professional" is entitled to a "new career," one in which she is complementary with and "equal" to mental health professionals, and one which permits advancement on the basis of skills and training. At any rate, clear specific training goals for mental health workers have to be developed for specific purposes. We would like to help develop both generalists and specialists, liberally exploiting (in a positive sense) the potential of many members of a community. As an example, mature housewives from both the ghetto and suburbia may start out by volunteering their services and may eventually become full-time paid workers. The community itself, e.g., community colleges, now appears to be assuming some of the responsibility in developing training programs for mental health workers leading to a certificate or degree and, most importantly, to competence.

The main requirements for a mental health worker are still that she be compassionate, that she like people, and that she be able to relate to and work with them. She is trained to be a "helping person"—a person who cares, a person who identifies with an individual in crisis, a person who can help others restate their problems and sift out the important aspects. The mental health worker is a responsible person who has a responsible job to perform.

Adults tend to envy adolescents because adolescents have not *yet* wasted their opportunities. Let us not waste ours!!